Ready or Not

2000

27TH EDITION

INSIDE YOU'LL FIND:

BY

SUZANNE ARNOLD
Ph.D. Florida State University
Educator and counselor for the aged

JEANNE BROCK
Adult educator and aging specialist

JIM CAULDER
Social Security specialist
Informed Decisions

LOWELL LEDFORD
Florida Department of Education

HENRY RICHARDS
Older workers specialist
Florida State Employment Service

SHIRLEY WILE
University of Wisconsin professor of
Educational Gerontology
and Retirement Planning

Artwork by Bill Kresse

Copyright © 2000 by Elizabeth M. McFadden, Twenty-Seventh Edition
Published by Manpower Education Institute. All rights reserved.
Manufactured in the United States of America
Library of Congress ISSN 1091-7268

Manpower Education Institute • 715 Ladd Road, Bronx, NY 10471-1203 • (718) 548-4200
fax: (718) 548-4202 • e-mail: meiready@aol.com • www.manpower-education.org

HOW DO I STAND?

(Yes)	(No)	
❑	❑	I know approximately what my social security income will be in retirement.
❑	❑	I know my pension benefits in retirement.
❑	❑	I have a financial savings plan for retirement.
❑	❑	I know approximately future income from my investments—IRA and savings.
❑	❑	I have completed a net worth statement.
❑	❑	I have analyzed my cash flow—monthly and yearly.
❑	❑	I have discussed finances with my spouse.
❑	❑	I have an up-to-date will.
❑	❑	I have a power-of-attorney on myself.
❑	❑	I have my important papers—including my will—where my family can find them. I have reviewed the papers with my spouse.
❑	❑	I have a regular exercise program.
❑	❑	I had a physical examination in the past year.
❑	❑	I've checked my health insurance coverage, both now and for retirement.
❑	❑	I've checked my home for safety and maintenance.
❑	❑	I've discussed retirement plans—where to live, what to do with time—with my spouse.
❑	❑	I am involved in at least one social activity—politics, volunteer work, civic and church activities.
❑	❑	I plan to continue learning after retirement.

THE TIME OF YOUR LIFE

Today, more than ever before, "aging" is an opportunity, not a problem. Americans in general are living longer, healthier, more active lives.

As you reach this plateau, you have the chance to pursue your happiness...without the responsibility or demands of work. And you have the energy and resources to achieve personal goals of travel, hobbies, education.

Have you prepared yourself and your family for this new opportunity? This book is designed to help you look clearly and positively at the changes and decisions of retirement. From Financial Planning to Health to Family Matters, or a new job, full or part-time, we address clearly and directly the financial, physical and emotional concerns you may have about retirement.

AN "AGING" NATION

The first thing to know about "aging" in America is that "everybody's doing it." The first of the 76 million Baby Boomers turned 50 in 1996. Between now and 2030, the aged will become a dominant segment of America's population.

People are living longer than ever before. In 1900, average life expectancy was 50 years. In 1960, the average 65-year-old American could expect to live another 18 years. Today, the average

length of retirement beyond 65 is 20 years.

Better health care, nutrition awareness, shorter work weeks, higher standard of living, earlier retirement...all have contributed to longer, more vibrant lives, affirming Browning's lines, "Come, grow old with me, the best is yet to come."

SOONER OR LATER

You may be reading this book and saying "I will not be retiring for sometime in the future." Think again. With downsizing, early retirement programs, buyouts, more and more of us are facing a choice sooner than anticipated.

Much of the information covered in *Ready or Not* is relevant at all ages and stages at work... and, as the title suggests, is intended to make you aware of the need to start planning for your future *today*.

READY OR NOT

Ready or Not is designed to help you make your future years satisfying, enriching and comfortable. Each chapter deals with issues of importance. Experts and professionals have contributed specific, detailed information in clear, concise language that will answer your questions about retirement.

Checklists and charts make it easy to pinpoint

AGING: DID YOU KNOW THAT?

- ❏ Senior citizens over 65 constitute 12.8% of the total U.S. population. More than 33.5 million persons, age 65 years or older, live in the United States.

- ❏ The ability to learn new skills and acquire new information remains relatively unchanged from age 20 through age 60. Intellectual powers do not decline as rapidly as people think. "You can't teach an old dog new tricks" is true only if the "old dog" happens to believe this proverb!

- ❏ Physical strength is maintained from biological maturity until age 60. Physical strength may be due to factors more related to health than to the number of years a person has lived.

- ❏ Comprehension and vocabulary ability holds strong through age 60. Physical dexterity and reaction to stimuli reach a peak at age 18 with a slow decline after age 40. Ability to learn, though, is relatively unaffected by age.

- ❏ Of all married couples over 65, the percentage living in their own households is 80%. For those individuals not married, 50% live on their own.

- ❏ The percentage of all persons over 65, living in an institution, is only 5%. Institutions include nursing homes, retirement homes, and mental hospitals.

- ❏ The average couple has 25 years of partial leisure after their children are grown.

- ❏ 90% of persons over 65 report relative freedom from chronic health problems that could limit their activities. Two factors that are important to extended health and happiness are: (1) an understanding of one's self (physically, mentally, and socially) and (2) good medical care in early and later life.

- ❏ About 75% of pre-retirement income is necessary to enable the retired person to maintain his previous level of spending and living. Some expenses will decrease: work-related expenses (eating out, clothes, transportation) and taxes will be lower. Housing may be lower, depending on where you will live. Bad news: inflation will affect buying power and health expenses will rise.

areas of major concern or interest to you. *Ready or Not* can be your guide to making the most of what can be the best years of your life; years in which you can truly appreciate your family, your friends, travel, hobbies, or just "giving back" to your community through volunteering.

RETIRING WELL

Many couples enter retirement without understanding each other's retirement dreams. Nor do they discuss openly what adjustments they expect to make when their partner retires.

It's especially important to discuss and plan the impact of retirement on your spouse, children, and siblings, and if your not married with your close relatives and friends. Retirement should be about retiring to something, not retire from something. Planning together will result in days filled with purpose and meaning. It's retiring well.

AGING GRACEFULLY

Every important phase of your life has been successful in proportion to the time and care you have invested: from education to career to marriage and family.

Surprises are fun for parties, but in daily life, as in business, surprises are usually not good news.

The first step to enjoying retirement is to take a close personal inventory.

❑ How is my health? Regular checkups, early attention to potential problems can save you money and give you more years of active healthy living.

❑ Am I financially ready for retirement? Since you probably won't win Lotto, a realistic look at your financial situation is crucial. Discuss finances openly with your family— financial planning is easier if it's shared.

❑ What will I do in retirement? This is where

preparation really pays off. Whether you plan to travel extensively, master a new skill, or get a degree, the door of opportunity is open wide. Mature Americans are going back to school in record numbers; retirement with planning can let you enjoy leisure as never before.

❑ Can I still contribute to society? Your experience and acquired knowledge make you invaluable to dozens of social, religious, civic organizations...and you have the time!

RETIREMENT OPTIONS

The concept of 65 as a retirement age appeared when the average American did not live that long. Our literature tells us that 50 was old age into the 1930's.

We are not only living longer, but youthful vigor and mental activity are also being extended.

According to a University of Michigan survey almost 75% of those between 51 and 61 prefer a gradual phasing down to part-time work.

Retirement income may not be sufficient in itself to meet your needs, whether they are financial or lifestyle related. Many retirees find alternative work options from home-office to part-time, or flex-time work situations.

Just as the 20th Century brought us the 40-hour, 5-day work week, so the 21st Century will see a redefinition of work and the workplace.

STAY YOUNG AT HEART

"You don't lose your enthusiasm when you get old. You get old because you lose your enthusiasm....stay enthusiastic, keep thinking, cherish high ideals and celebrate life with your family and friends."

– Reverend Calvin Butts, Senior Minister
Abyssinian Baptist Church

YOUR FINANCIAL FUTURE

Where do you stand? Are you a young person just entering the business world? At the midpoint of your career? Rapidly approaching retirement? Whatever your situation it makes good sense to regularly review your financial status thoroughly, and do some sound and intensive planning for the future. This section will help you do just that. A rich, rewarding life doesn't happen by accident. Whatever your personal/family goals, the best means of achieving them is through planning: financial, career...all aspects of life.

PLANNING IS VITAL

Without planning, family funds may be spent in a thoughtless and wasteful way. There's never much left for savings and investment, and necessary but perhaps careless borrowing burdens us with expensive interest.

A careless approach to family finances makes life more difficult. There are always major financial needs looming that may further complicate matters:

The need for a new furnace, a new car or a new house; children and their own special needs, often costly ones; particularly college educations; and finally, too soon, retirement—often 15 to 20 years of living without that full monthly paycheck.

INFLATION'S IMPACT

Inflation is an insidious thing. We know it is happening, but we don't give sufficient attention to the effect it has on every dollar we earn and save. Between 1968 and 1988 we in the United States experienced inflation *every* year, varying from 1.5% to a double-digit figure of 13.5%. The real shocker is that in this 20-year period the Consumer Price Index went from 104 to 347.6— *a total increase of 234%.*

The Consumer Price Index from the third quarter of 1998 to the third quarter of 1999 rose 2.4%. This is the base for determining Social Security payments in 2000. Good news, even at this low rate, the purchasing power of a year-2000 dollar will decline to 60 cents in twenty years. While financial advisors say it costs less to live in retirement—75% of preretirement income— using 3% inflation going forward, a family with an income of $40,000 today will need a retirement income of approximately $72,245 in the year 2020 to live comfortably. More, if inflation increases.

TWO KEYS TO PLANNING

A sound financial plan is crucial to insure comfortable living for you and yours, as a safeguard against personal needs, crises and inflation. This section outlines how to develop such a plan focusing on two important elements:

❑ Controlling family expenditures by evaluating current spending practices and developing a practical and effective family budget program.

❑ Insuring an adequate level of future income by setting up a consistent, diversified and balanced investment plan.

Note: At the end of this chapter, you will find worksheets for computing your cash flow and net worth.

THE FIRST STEP

The first step is to start developing a personal financial plan. It is important to determine your current financial status so that you can develop a long-range plan to help achieve your financial goals. Primarily this involves computing your net worth. Your net worth is simply the difference between your assets and your liabilities.

YOUR NET WORTH

This computation tells you whether or not your assets (cash, bank accounts, stock, etc.) exceed your liabilities (mortgage, charge cards, etc.)— and by how much. It also tells you what percentage the total value of your assets is represented by each category. It provides you with a similar analysis of your liabilities.

With this information you can evaluate your current financial condition in a thorough and systematic way. Review the figures, asking the questions:

- ❑ Do I have a major financial problem with my assets barely exceeding my liabilities?

- ❑ Is my life insurance adequate for my family's needs?

- ❑ Do I have sufficient money set aside in liquid funds for our current needs?

- ❑ Are my investments properly planned and diversified?

- ❑ Can I depend on being paid the full value of my loans receivable?

Similar questions can and should be asked about the composition of liabilities you have listed. They represent, in most instances, heavy finance charges that should be minimized as much and as quickly as possible.

PAPERS YOU'LL NEED

To start, gather all your financial papers and reports that provide information on your assets and liabilities. These will include such items as: savings records, checkbooks, statements for CD's, stocks, bonds, funds, etc. and similar reports on your residence, vehicles, mortgages, loans, etc.

Hopefully, you have all these papers put aside in one place and organized for easy reference. If they are not so organized, this is an opportunity to correct the situation for future reference.

Also it's not that hard to locate the market value of some of the listed items. Tax reports and records can be helpful, and a check of the classified section of your local paper can give you a good idea of the value of such assets as your home, your cars, tools and equipment, etc.

RICHER...OR POORER?

It is a good idea to perform a net worth computation yearly, so that you can see how your net worth is growing. In evaluating this growth, look for two things:

- ❑ A steady growth from year to year.

- ❑ A growth rate that exceeds the inflation rate by a substantial amount.

If the growth rate is low or uneven, compare this current year's net worth computation alongside last year's and determine any areas of weakness. How are your investments growing in value? Your real estate? Are your liabilities being reduced? Your loan indebtedness? Mortgage obligations?

Effective use of the net worth computation and trend analysis is an important first step in gaining a better understanding of your family's financial condition.

YOUR CASH FLOW

If a look at your net worth (and the trend in its growth—or decline) suggests something needs to be done to improve your financial status the best way to get a precise understanding of the problem is to compare your *expenses* versus your *income* in a specific way. The "worksheet for computing your cash flow" (page 25) will help you do this.

Determining your cash flow shows you whether or not your expenses exceed your income—or vice versa. If expenses exceed income and you are losing ground financially, obviously you need to take corrective action. If, on the other hand, expenses and income balance out, then the question is whether or not sufficient funds are being set aside for savings and investment.

However, let's assume that the totals as shown clearly indicate you are overspending. You will need to look at the individual items in your "expenses" listing to determine areas in which the spending problem is centered. Probably these areas will stand out "like a sore thumb."

SPENDING PATTERNS

It is very helpful to compare the percentage of income you spend on each category with a break-down the following budget for the "average" retired couple (source: the Bureau of Labor Statistics):

Housing	33%
Food	29%
Transportation	10%
Medical Care	10%
Clothing	5%
Personal Care	3%
Entertainment & Education	4%
Other	6%

If your percentages vary widely from the above, this is another clue to the categories in which you may be overspending.

DETERMINING CASH FLOW

This takes some doing. So give yourself adequate time to do the job right.

Use the "expenses" listing on the form as your initial guide taking one category at a time to find the needed information. Much of this information can be obtained from your checkbook, your credit card statements or your tax records.

The most difficult information to get involves cash purchases. Either estimate these figures from personal experience, or keep a journal on these items for several weeks to establish a spending pattern.

Income information should be detailed in a similar way, using your income statements for reference purposes.

Important: *Don't expect to achieve perfect accuracy with this analysis. Even an imperfect job will give you a strong starting point for understanding and improving your financial status.*

WHAT NEXT?

If you have just completed the Cash Flow Worksheet, you know whether your expenses exceed your income. If they do, you need to take some immediate action to correct this imbalance and start saving for the future.

Even if your income exceeds expenses, it's still a good idea to evaluate and control family spending practices. Do this conscientiously and use the extra funds to further beef up your savings and investments.

Cutting back on expenses is not as difficult as you might think. Most of us have let items once considered luxuries become necessities. This becomes apparent if we study closely the different elements of our expenses. A $20 savings here—$10 there—an occasional $40-$50 savings, can add up to $150 to $250 monthly, a tidy sum to help in the balancing process.

EXAMINE YOUR SPENDING

Look at your listing of "expenses" The list covers practically all the ways you can spend your hard-earned income. So take each category; study it carefully—one item at a time.

Take plenty of time and thoroughly evaluate the expenditures made for each item. Be sure to ask yourself the right questions:

❑ Is (this) product or service really essential?

❑ Could we get by with a less sophisticated, less expensive version of the item?

❑ Are we using more of the product or service than we really need?

❑ Are we buying at a good, competitive price?

YOUR ACTION PLAN

Follow-up your review with a written action plan. As you study each category, decide what, if any, reduction plan you want to implement and note it under the appropriate heading in the action plan.

Obviously, you can't implement all reductions at once; so prioritize reductions, putting the most significant first in line. Set a deadline for completion of each one. This puts some pressure on you to make your plan work.

Start taking the actions called for—handling one item at a time. Take your time and do each job right. Then, as you complete each action, cross it off your list.

When you have completed this balancing of your expenses and income, you will be ready for the next step—setting up your budget.

A COOPERATIVE PROJECT

You will probably find that many of the expense reduction measures you decide upon will not penalize anyone in the family. However, if the out-of-balance financial condition is a serious

LIBRARY: AN INFORMATION RESOURCE

As you go through your listing of expenses you may say to yourself, "I need more information about that"—or—"What are the alternatives to the way we are handling this matter?" This is the study and research part of the job that helps you achieve the reduction results you want.

There is a source nearby that greatly simplifies any research job—your public library. Books and periodicals cover every conceivable subject— including the ones in your expenses listing:

Ideas on how to save on taxes; tips on reducing house mortgage payments; insurance information; buying guide; economy food tips and menus; etc.

With the help of the librarian you can quickly become an expert at locating whatever you want to know about the elements in your listing of expenses.

one, more drastic measures must be taken. The decisions reached on such reductions should be agreed to with good humor by both husband and wife—with the rest of the family also having input.

MORTGAGE SAVINGS

We've taken the "housing" account and gone through it for you—just as you might do it yourself:

"Okay," you might say to yourself, "These are big budget items. Can we save on them, starting with the mortgage payments?

"Well, interest rates have been bouncing around for the past year or so. It may be possible to refinance—lowering the interest rate we're paying. Sure, there will be costs involved in the switch, but in the long run we may be able to save thousands of dollars on interest charges.

"Also, haven't people been talking about

saving money on their mortgage by just 'paying ahead'? We could ask about that too."

The next question you'll ask is, "Are we getting the right coverage and a good price on our homeowner's insurance?

"First, we're going to take a closer look at our policy and be sure we understand all the provisions— and coverages; check on whether or not they provide the protection we want: not too little—but not too much either. That's costly. Then we'll check with a few friends to see what their homeowner's costs them. Maybe—after we've done a little research at the library—we'll get a couple of proposals from different insurance companies, too. Might be able to save some money on the premiums.

MORTGAGE MATH

Here is an example of the difference between monthly and biweekly payments on a 30-year $50,000 mortgage at 8% interest.

	Monthly	Biweekly
Payment	$368	$184
Annually	$4,416	$4,784
Total interest paid until maturity	$82,480	$47,336
Years to maturity	30 years	20 years, 9 months

"And we're going to check out carefully the other house expenditures we make. The little odd jobs—maybe we can learn to do more of them ourselves.

"Now let's make some notes on these matters in our expense reduction action plan."

Note: If you take every category in your listing of expenses and go through them in this way, you can be sure of this: unless you were the neighborhood's greatest efficiency expert you will find a lot of savings possibilities that will help you do your "balancing act" without fear or pain.

SET UP A BUDGET

If you have been developing a financial plan along the lines we have been suggesting, you have examined your spending habits, planned projected adjustments in that spending pattern, and set up, in effect, a yearly spending budget by category.

Put this planned spending pattern in a budget form that you can use to control your spending and achieve your financial goals.

WHY A BUDGET?

Beside the obvious advantages of eliminating waste and controlling expenditures, there are a number of additional advantages to living by a budget:

❑ Having a budget makes the task of achieving financial security much easier. It is a road map, helping you reach your objective with fewer delays and wrong turns.

❑ You know where you stand financially from month to month.

❑ It helps generate money for that all-important investment program that will enable you to meet major expenses down the line (home, children, college, retirement).

SOME OVERALL TIPS

Many people have given up on budgets because they didn't use good judgment in setting them up in the first place. To avoid this, consider the following suggestions as outlined by many financial planners:

❑ Continue to approach your working budget as a family project with husband and wife— and the children, too—having input. If decisions are not made on a truly mutual and fair basis, family members just won't work to make the project succeed.

❑ Keep the budget format—and the necessary administration of the program—as simple as possible. As you go along, you may find ways to eliminate unnecessary details or record-keeping. Don't forget your primary objective—and the importance of "knowing where you stand."

❑ Accept the first few months as a trial-and-error period. Evaluate what you are doing carefully—making necessary adjustments in allocations and in the way you keep records.

KEEPING BUDGET RECORDS

"Standard budget books" are available at every office supply store. Many of them are well-designed and instructions for their use are spelled out in detail. Examine these budget books, carefully selecting the one that suits your style. One feature in particular to look for is a thorough breakdown and listing of the various possible types of expenditures. You need such a listing so you will know which accounts to charge for the wide variety of expenses you incur.

You can also use the format from the "Cash Flow Worksheet" in this section to set up your budget record on a columnar pad. However, it's a good idea to refer to one of the "standard books" in setting up the category listings, the method of recording information, and the structure for summarizing expenditures.

YOUR SPENDING: KEEP TRACK

Whichever budget book you select, the format of the monthly record will be reasonably self-explanatory. There will probably be a good set of instructions on how to make the necessary entries and computations. However, here are a few suggestions which may further simplify the process for you.

❑ If you look at the budget accounts, you will see it is very easy to obtain much of the information asked for. It is shown either in your checkbook record or credit card statement. Transfer the appropriate information to your budget record once a month. Recognize the value of a checkbook record as a source of budget information.

❑ Other expenses include the frequent cash purchases for food, entertainment, personal care, etc. Some plan must be set up to keep track of these expenditures. One way is to keep receipts for all cash purchases, checking to be sure they show clearly the items purchased and the prices paid.

❑ Where no receipt is provided, keep a listing in a notebook you carry for that purpose. With these notes it is easy to update your budget record.

❑ Another control on small item purchases is the business "Purchase Order" approach.

Establish a limit on an item, such as "meals out" and limit spending to that level. Try this, and you'll watch your nickels and dimes. This makes it easy to record the total of these expenditures in your budget book. It's the budget amount shown—or less.

YOUR BUDGET AT WORK

Keeping your budget program working is the last and most important factor in the process. This starts with a clear assignment of responsibilities.

- ❑ Who is going to be responsible for keeping the budget records? This must be specified so the job gets done regularly.

- ❑ How is responsibility for controlling different categories of spending to be divided between husband and wife? The cash purchases for food, entertainment, personal care and miscellaneous items are a particular problem here. You should look at this matter together, using recent experience as your guide—and make a list of the specific items for which each will be responsible.

WHERE TO KEEP YOUR MONEY

Where do you keep the budget funds so they are safe—yet readily available? Some will choose a joint checking account; others a savings account *and* a checking account. Separate checking accounts are a third way. With this system, an appropriate allocation of monthly income is made to each account to cover assigned expenditures. Each spouse draws on "his" or "her" account as needed during the month, for cash or to pay current bills by check. Whatever system you decide on, make the plan concrete and follow the agreed-upon procedure to avoid any misunderstanding between partners.

Finally, there is the very important monthly budget review. This review determines whether or not your program works. At this review you and your partner check whether or not you are staying within budget limits. If not, decide what action to take to stop overspending— account by account. If you are underspending in some categories, you can adjust upward the budget limits in other account categories as good judgment advises.

A budget program as outlined here, will provide reasonable assurance that you are spending your income wisely, and in line with your preferences. Also, if you have planned well, you will know that allocations are being made regularly to your investment account, to insure continued financial security.

INVESTING

We now move ahead to another important phase of our financial planning. We have set aside funds for savings and investments of some kind. The amount in your budget for this purpose may be small, but hopefully it will increase as you add a portion of your future cost-of-living and merit pay increases to the funds designated for savings.

You need to develop a plan for utilizing these funds effectively. Such a plan should provide for current, day-to-day living expenses and the minimizing of credit card and loan debt—and make a start on setting aside money for such major family requirements as: home, children, advanced education, and, ultimately, retirement.

This section covers the alternatives available for such savings and investment purposes and how to structure such a program. There are three phases, in line with the way such a program realistically is developed:

- ❑ First phase: setting aside an adequate "working fund" and essential insurance protection.

- ❑ Second phase: starting a savings program to provide added financial protection and coverage of future needs.

- ❑ Third phase: developing a full-blown savings and investment plan.

JUST IN CASE...

As the heading suggests, at the start of your financial planning you should take care of two prime financial needs: a "working fund"—and insurance protection. We'll begin with...

THE WORKING FUND

Every family needs such a fund. It provides for your day-to-day expenses and also should be large enough to cover such major expenses as: car repairs, all but the largest appliance purchases, even such emergencies as a temporary lay-off. These funds should be readily available. Still—even at this first stage—you want this fund to be earning "something" in the form of interest.

The problem of "credit card" and other debt appears at this point. Some people seem to think that having a credit card—or two—or *more,* somehow *increases* their income. Of course, it doesn't—just the opposite. Rather than saving you money, it costs you a whopping 18-20% in interest each year. Yet the use of a credit card for borrowing purposes becomes a habit. The required monthly payment seems small, and more and more debt accumulates. Having a number of cards and a total credit card balance of $2,000 or more is quite common.

CREDIT CARD DANGERS

This is a dangerous financial situation. It has become a real problem for you when you start to see tell-tale signs such as these: You never have adequate funds to start paying down the balance on your credit cards. You must use a credit card to borrow money to meet day-to-day living expenses. You take out a new credit card to borrow money to make the payments on your current cards.

Here's an example that highlights the folly of using credit cards carelessly:

- ❏ Suppose you save $2,000 and put it in a savings account earning 3% interest. You will earn $60 per year on your savings.
- ❏ Suppose, on the other hand, you put aside $2,000 and paid off the $2,000 balance on your credit card. You would save—in effect earn—18% on the transaction, or $360. That's $300 more than the $60 you would earn on $2,000 in a 3% savings account.

The rule of thumb is to never use credit to pay for everyday living expenses. Use credit to buy assets that have long term value: a home, a car, a major appliance that reduces living expenses.

Back to the "working fund." Obviously such a fund helps you avoid excessive credit card and loan indebtedness. The question is: "How much should you have in such a fund?" Financial planners seem to agree you should keep about two-to-three months income in such a fund. That is:

- ❏ With a $2,500 monthly income: a fund of $5,000-$7,500
- ❏ With a $3,500 monthly income: a fund of $7,000-$10,500

As to where you keep these funds, the alternatives are probably familiar to you and are mostly available from your local bank or credit union. Make sure these savings alternatives guarantee security of your funds either by the FDIC or the NCUA and your account totals less than the stipulated limit for liability.

STRUCTURING YOUR SAVINGS

As suggested, you want adequate liquid funds available as needed, but you want to be earning some interest too. Divide your "working fund" between: your checking account, and either a savings account or a money management account.

Keep just enough in your checking to meet current monthly needs—and the rest in the money management account, earning interest. Watch closely the balance between accounts to be sure you are earning interest on as much of your fund as possible.

DO YOU NEED A FINANCIAL PLANNER?

Although financial planners can help you make investment decisions, hiring a planner presumes you have discretionary income to invest. Experts say most investments should not be made until you have financed very basic living items, such as housing, insurance, and a cash reserve fund for emergencies. If you find you cannot meet these (and other) necessary financial requirements, you may decide you need help not in investment planning, but in basic money management.

Whether or not you use the services of a financial planner you must organize by preparing your own net-worth and cash-flow worksheets.

Be informed on financial matters. Your library is a great source and your local educational institutions offer classes. Do this whether or not you hire a financial planner.

If you have money to invest and decide you need a financial planner, ask about payment method. **Be Careful**. Some "planners" are salespersons for products they recommend. Fee-only planners charge a straight fee for their services. Get a written statement of their charges.

Ask for a sample of a written financial plan.

INSURANCE PROTECTION

If you're married and have a family, you must realize the need for insurance protection, in the event some unforeseen tragedy should befall you or your spouse. This need is greatest when you are younger, and the insurance benefit must provide income for your family over a long span of years.

The need for such protection should lessen as you grow older. Over the years, you and your spouse should build assets that provide income protection. Your children will grow up, become independent, and become self sufficient.

Set up your life insurance program *early* as part of your financial base. Plan to provide adequate financial protection, particularly at the start.

The type of money managers you and your spouse are determines to a great extent the type of insurance plan that is best for you:

❑ If you have the discipline and control necessary to handle such a plan, many financial planners would say you should select an ample "term" policy, putting any additional money that is available into such investment as a sound mutual fund.

❑ If you don't have the discipline for consistent contributions to a separate savings and investment program, then you are better off with a universal life or variable life program. With this approach, you are, in effect, forced to make the regular investments as a means of keeping the policy in force.

HOW MUCH PROTECTION?

Few people can afford to buy sufficient insurance protection to guarantee that their families will not suffer a loss of income at the death or disability of the major wage earner. Instead, do the best you can with the money available for this purpose.

The first thing to do in this matter is to consider what income the family would have considering such factors as: the earning ability of the surviving spouse, the current state of the family finances, the possibility and level of Social Security benefits.

Set up your insurance plan to come as close as possible to the monthly income needed for reasonably comfortable living.

DISABILITY INSURANCE

You're twice as likely to be disabled for 90 days as to die before age 65. Yet fewer than half of all working adults have disability insurance.

You and your spouse need enough coverage to maintain 60 to 70 percent of your current family income if either of you becomes disabled. Group coverage through your employer is cheapest. If that's not available, try to get a group rate through a group to which you belong.

The older you are when you apply for disability insurance, the higher the cost. You can lower costs by stretching the elimination period. A policy that starts payments on Day 90 of disability will cost 40 percent less than one that pays on Day 30.

CASH VALUE LIFE INSURANCE

As we have just discussed, the newer forms of life insurance—variable life, for example—have better investment potential than whole life policies. Assuming the investments do well, that is. So, should you consider switching? While there are cost and legal implications, a better question is, "Do you still need the insurance, and is that need likely to last for your lifetime?"

Remember that most of the reasons why people have insurance go away with time. For example, child-raising, debt payoffs and spouse protection. And when that insurance need stops, what remains is the cash value, or the investment.

Investing in an insurance policy is expensive. Agent commissions, state premium taxes,

---

INSURANCE OPTIONS

Term Insurance. Term insurance provides the greatest dollar amount of coverage for the least amount of money—$100,000 of protection for just several hundred dollars per year. However, the premiums for a specific amount of insurance become greater as you grow older. Since your needs for such protection grow less too, you can reduce the amount of your coverage as you see fit. Term insurance does not build any cash value.

Whole Life. This insurance provides a stipulated death benefit, but it also includes a savings feature, building cash value as the years go by. You can borrow against this cash value: and if you eventually cancel the policy—cash it in, obtaining the savings that have built up. The chief problem with this type of policy is the low rate of interest usually earned in the savings phase of the plan. (Universal life is similar to whole life but ordinarily provides a better return on the savings portion of the policy because of the way the savings funds are invested.)

Variable Life. This type of insurance combines the features of a whole life policy with those of a mutual fund. Be careful before purchasing. Their are commissions, annual charges, penalties for early withdrawal and severance fees in many of the policies. Understand the policy, check with your banker, credit union or lawyer for advice. Resist high pressure sales pitches.

required reserves and so forth, all reduce the investment. And none are present in, say, no-load mutual funds. Other things being equal, lower costs mean greater returns.

So before you continue your whole life policy, or consider switching to a "newer" contract, think about whether a term policy combined with a no-load fund might be better.

YOUR SAVINGS PROGRAM

The purpose of starting a savings and investment program is to provide financial security as the years go by—particularly in retirement. As we have emphasized, inflation makes this a particularly difficult goal to achieve.

BUILDING A RETIREMENT FUND

Let's look at two examples of how a retirement fund can build over the years through the magic of compound interest. You will note that in addition to the regular contributions to the plan—all earnings are also reinvested as the years go by.

Looking at these two examples you can see that even a relatively modest amount of monthly savings quickly grows into a substantial fund that can provide added income in your retirement years. The chart also shows that even a few added points of interest on your investments (6% to 9%) substantially increases the growth of such a fund.

	Number of years	Amount Each year	Total invested	Total Investing plus Earnings
Plan A	1-5	$1,000	$5,000	$5,975.33
6%	6-10	2,000	15,000	19,946.97
Compound	11-15	3,000	30,000	44,619.02
Interest	16-20	3,000	45,000	77,635.50
	21-25	3,000	60,000	121,819.75
Plan B	1-5	$1,000	$5,000	$6,523.33
9%	6-10	2,000	15,000	22,000.81
Compound	11-15	3,000	30,000	53,421.73
Interest	16-20	3,000	45,000	101,765.96
	21-25	3,000	60,000	172,585.22

HOW LONG WILL YOUR MONEY LAST?

This chart shows you how long your capital will last if you withdraw a fixed amount each year. * means it will last indefinitely at that rate.

Percentage of capital withdrawn yearly	Years money will last if invested at these rates:					
	5%	6%	7%	8%	9%	10%
8%	21	24	31	*	*	*
10%	15	16	18	21	27	*
12%	11	12	13	15	17	19
14%	10	10	11	12	12	14
16%	8	9	9	10	10	11
18%	7	7	8	8	9	9
20%	6	7	7	7	7	8

In considering these examples, you must remember that the results shown do not reflect the effect of any income tax requirements, a factor which could severely effect the growth in appreciation shown. This calls attention to the value of an investment approach that takes advantage of any tax-free or tax-deferred investments available.

Every person or family should have some type of savings or investment program. It may involve only a modest contribution; but these contributions are made consistently into a carefully selected, tax-efficient investment that provides a decent return and appreciation.

When you talk about setting up a savings and investment program, you discover people fall into two categories:

❑ Either they work for a business or other type of organization, or

❑ They are self-employed.

Let's consider the investment approach appropriate to each of these groups.

WORKING FOR A BUSINESS

There are two approaches you can use to make your "beginning" savings and investment program tax-efficient:

❑ Participation in your company retirement program.

❑ Use of an Individual Retirement Account (IRA).

YOUR EMPLOYER'S PROGRAM

Employer retirement programs vary widely, but a typical program might very well include:

Life, accident and disability insurance, a non-contributory and contributory pension plan, a company savings and stock investment plan and more.

The advantage of such employer programs are numerous including the fact they provide the tax-efficient approach that is so important to decent growth in your investment savings. This applies to both the Simplified Employee Pension (SEP) and to the so-called 401 (k) plans. In some instances your initial contributions to these plans are excluded from your earnings before income taxes are withheld. Usually earnings on all types of contributions are sheltered from income taxes while they are held in the plan and until they are withdrawn.

In addition to the tax advantages of such a plan, employer contributions often make the plans doubly attractive. The employer usually covers many of the required program costs: the non-contributory part of the pension plan, the full cost of some phases of the insurance program, a sizeable percentage add-on for every dollar saved and invested by an employee participant (half a dollar or more in many instances). Just think:

A modest $200 monthly contribution to the employer stock program may qualify for a $100 or more matching contribution by the employer for a total of $300 monthly— $3,600 per year.

Because of the advantages of your employer program, you should make every effort to participate using the funds set aside in your budget for such a program.

YOUR EMPLOYER'S RETIREMENT PROGRAM: FACTORS TO CONSIDER

❑ Study the employer retirement brochure carefully to be sure you understand all the benefits available to you. Study the details, too, so you know the key rights and restrictions pertaining to each of these benefits. For example, there probably will be restrictions or penalties for withdrawal from the fund. On the other hand, you may be able to borrow against your investments in an emergency and avoid such penalties.

❑ Consider the savings funds you have available monthly and carefully select the type of investments you prefer. Perhaps you start with participation in the contributory phase of the pension plan, an approach which earns good returns and helps insure that your basic "pension" at retirement is ample for your needs. You might put any additional funds available in the stock investment plan.

❑ A number of employers are adapting cash balance pension plans instead of traditional pension programs. These plans are advantageous to younger workers who may change jobs frequently and can take a lump sum payment when they leave the employer. Employers also save money. For older workers, unless the company continues them in the old plan, as many do, there is a significant drop in pension benefits. Check your plan. Congress, government agencies and the courts are examining these plans. Stay tuned.

LUMP SUM DISTRIBUTIONS

If you have participated in a plan like a 401(k) plan, or any other qualified retirement plan, you may have the option of receiving a lump-sum distribution upon retirement.

A lump-sum distribution is usually the entire balance in your retirement savings plan. Since this could be a large sum, you should consult a tax advisor to help you decide among the available options.

Basically, you can take the distribution as ordinary income and pay taxes on it the year it is received (no tax is due on your after-tax contributions). Or, you can defer taxation by rolling over all or part of the money into an Individual Retirement Account (IRA). Other alternatives for your distribution include: keeping it invested in stock, buying an Individual Retirement Annuity, or leaving it in your employer's plan.

In determining the best course of action, consider the amount of the distribution, how soon you need the money, other resources available to you, your age, health, and anticipated investment return.

Option 1: TAKE CASH

You have the option to take the entire lump sum in cash. This is not the best option. Taxes must be paid on the amount received (excluding any after-tax contributions). If you are under 59 ½, you may incur a 10% penalty for early withdrawal.

Employers must withhold 20% from eligible rollover distributions for federal income taxes unless the money is directly rolled over to an IRA or another qualified retirement plan.

You may be able to minimize your tax bite. It becomes complicated. Consult with a tax accountant before you take the money.

Option 2: ROLL OVER INTO AN IRA

You can defer paying income taxes on all or part of a lump sum distribution by reinvesting the money in an IRA through a direct or indirect rollover. (After-tax contributions cannot be rolled over.)

In order to avoid having 20% of your distribution withheld, however, you should request a direct rollover to an IRA (Trust to Trust). With this approach, you instruct your employer to directly roll your distribution into an IRA rather than pay the money to you. Make sure it is payable to the custodian of your new IRA. Otherwise, the distribution will be subject to the 20% withholding and maybe penalties.

If the distribution is paid to you, you can still do an indirect rollover in which you have 60 days to reinvest the money in an IRA. However, even if you roll over the total amount received, you will pay income taxes, as well as a possible 10% penalty if you're under age 59 ½, on the 20% of the distribution withheld by your employer. To avoid this, you must roll over the 20% from your own pocket.

A consideration with this option is, you must begin to take your distribution at age 70 ½. And, if your distribution was mostly in the form of stock you won't be able to pay capital gains rates when you sell the shares.

FINDING LOST PENSIONS

Are you due a pension, but your old employer has gone out of business and you don't know where to go to collect your money? Help is available from:

The Pension Benefit Guaranty Corporation
Missing Participant Program
1200 K Street N.W.
Washington, DC 20005
800-326-LOST
www.pbgc.gov.com

Include you name, address, daytime telephone number, Social Security number, date of birth and name and location of the employer, as well as the dates of your employment.

Also, if you have any documents issued by the plan, include the nine-digit Employer Identification Number and the three-digit Plan Identification Number that are often printed on such papers.

Option 3: KEEP THE STOCK

If your retirement plan consists mostly of highly appreciated stock it might be a good idea to keep the stock. You will owe taxes, but only on the value of the shares at the time you purchased them or when the company added them to your account. You can continue to defer taxes on all the share-price gains from the initial date of purchase until you sell the stock. You will pay annual income taxes on any dividends.

In doing this you convert what might have been ordinary income into long-term capital gain. Your heirs may fare better in this option as they will owe taxes only on the share-price gain of the stock prior to taking the shares out of the plan.

To find out how much you might save in taxes ask your employee benefits department to provide you with the "net unrealized appreciation" (NUA) on those shares before you make any withdrawals.

Option 4: TAKE A LIFETIME ANNUITY

Many plans offer to make annuity distributions. Should you desire an annuity it's probably a better value to obtain one through your employer's plan. Annuities are complicated. **Be careful!** They do offer for some, advantages, for others, they should not be purchased. There are sales commissions, fees and charges that vary widely and affect your return. Should you withdraw within a certain period, usually up to seven years most annuities have severance charges. For a withdrawal before 59 ½ under most circumstances there will be a 10% penalty on the interest you have earned. Learn all you can about annuities before purchasing.

Option 5: EMPLOYER'S PLAN

You may choose to leave the lump sum in your employer's plan. Check with your plan administrator. If they allow former participants to keep their accounts, the likely result is lower cost and thus higher returns. Remember, if you rollover your lump sum you become an individual investor and may encounter charges such as fees and commissions, two things normally not present in the employer's plan. Providing the employer's investments are acceptable, doing nothing may be a good choice, for now. But be aware that investments may be moved without your permission.

INDIVIDUAL RETIREMENT ACCOUNT

If your employer does not have a retirement program, you will want to make an IRA your first choice for the investment of your retirement savings. Even if you do have a company program, you probably will want to participate to the extent possible under the terms of the IRA plan—if you have the funds to do so.

Any of several different investments can be used for an IRA account. In setting up and participating in such a program, you will want to

IF YOU DON'T WAIT 'TILL LATER...   **YOUR YIELD WILL BE GREATER**

IRA TREE PLANTED AT AGE 55

IRA TREE PLANTED AT AGE 35

do your "homework" and base your decision on sound research and good judgment.

Generally, the younger you are, your investments should be geared to possible growth. The older person should be somewhat more conservative.

TRADITIONAL IRA

❑ A 1997 law increases the number of working taxpayers under the age of 70 to deduct IRA contributions from their income by doubling the income limits to $50,000 for singles by 2005 and to $80,000 for couples by 2007.

❑ Expands IRA opportunities for nonworking spouses by removing the income limitation on deductible contributions in families where only one spouse is covered by a pension plan.

ROTH IRA

The 1997 law created a new type of IRA, named after Senator Roth. The Roth IRA permits:

❑ Working taxpayers at any age with adjusted gross income below $95,000 if single or $150,00 if married, filing jointly to contribute up to $2000 per year for all IRAs combined. Contributions are not tax deductible.

❑ No taxes on investment gains for qualified withdrawals.

❑ Contributions can be withdrawn at any time without taxes or penalties. There are no penalties or taxes on earnings withdrawn after account has been open 5 years and after age

"HOW TO GET RICH" IN THE STOCK MARKET

Take all your savings and buy some stock and hold it till it goes up. If it don't go up, don't buy it.

Will Rogers
October, 1929

59 ½, death, disability or for certain home purchases (up to $10,000). There are taxes but no penalties on earnings withdrawn if made within 5 years of opening an account and for certain home purchases **or** made at any time for qualified higher education expenses.

EDUCATIONAL IRA

The1997 law created a Education IRA in which contributions up to $500 can be deposited in an Education IRA account. It is not tax deductible but withdrawals are tax free if used for qualified educational expenses. There is a 10% penalty for other non-qualified distributions.

IF YOU ARE SELF-EMPLOYED

You can take advantage of the tax-efficient benefits of what is called a Keogh plan. This plan is similar to an IRA, but is designed specifically for persons who work for themselves: doctors, dentists, store owners, accountants, freelance writers, etc. Sole proprietors and partners may set up a Keogh plan. There are certain legal requirements. You may want to see an accountant.

A tax deduction for contributions to a retirement plan and deferral of tax on income to the plan are benefits that apply to all self-employed persons (including owner-employees) who have a Keogh plan. The amount eligible for deduction is substantial but the formula varies with the specific type of Keogh plan involved. The maximum salary limitation is $160,000 (inflation adjusted) and the maximum deductible contribution ranges from 13.04% to 20% of salary, depending on the type of plan; profit sharing or money purchase.

BALANCED APPROACH

As mentioned under the discussion of IRA's, you probably—at the start—will want to take a balanced approach to your investments. Here are several types of investments you may want to consider because they provide reasonable safety and security, and usually provide an improved rate of earnings over savings accounts.

Certificates of Deposit. Certificates of Deposit provide insured security of principal (if they meet legal requirements). They also provide interest earnings at fixed or variable rates that are higher than those earned on savings accounts. The term of the Certificate (six months, one year, five years, etc.) usually affects the amount of interest earned.

Certificates of Deposit are not strictly liquid investments because of restrictions on withdrawals. But a portion of the funds invested can be made available at regular intervals by staggering maturity dates.

Bonds and Bond Funds. You can buy and sell individual bonds, but many investors find it less complicated to use mutual bond funds. These funds spread their investments over the bonds of many different companies and governmental organizations, thus providing the security that comes with diversification.

Bond funds usually are categorized into three groups: corporate, government, and tax-free municipals. Overall they are considered to be relatively low-risk investments, but they do not have guaranteed security in some cases.

Bond funds usually provide an attractive rate of return on your investment. However, the share value of bonds and bond funds, including government bond funds, fluctuate with interest rates: share value goes down when interest rates go up; and share values go up when interest rates go down.

Balanced Mutual Stock Funds and Growth and Income Funds. These funds seek both capital growth and dividend income through balanced investments in both stocks and bonds. They are not as risk-free as Certificates of Deposit or bond funds, but on the average generally provide a good return on your investments over a period of time.

Whatever type of investment you decide to use, you will want to emphasize certain approaches in carrying out your program.

❑ Select the funds and sources in which you plan to invest very carefully. That is, "comparison shop." Be particularly careful of fees and commissions.

❑ Make your yearly investment as large as possible considering the funds you have available.

❑ Make your contribution procedure as painless as possible by setting it up as an automatic payroll deduction, or as an automatic payment from your bank savings account.

LET'S REVIEW

Key factors in starting an investment program:

❑ Recognize fully the importance of using tax-efficient approaches for your savings and investment programs.

❑ Begin today so your investment program will have a maximum chance to grow through consistent contributions and the compounding of interest achieved by reinvesting all earnings as the years go by.

EXPANDING INVESTMENTS

The purpose of this phase of your investment planning is to increase your savings to the point that they will provide for the additional needs and preferences of the family: advanced education for the children, a better home, the possibility of travel now and in retirement.

Your personal situation at this point, ideally, is that your income from work has improved—or perhaps your spouse has gone to work as well. You continue to live on your budget (somewhat

SIMPLE SAVINGS STEPS...

❑ Take advantage of your pension plan, payroll deduction plan, 401 (k) salary deduction plan, deferred compensation plan.

❑ Have a separate savings account.

❑ Do not spend your next raise.

❑ If you get a tax refund or bonus, save it.

❑ Pay off your mortgage sooner by taking a 15-year loan, paying on a bi-weekly basis or making extra payments on the principal.

❑ Pay off credit cards to save the money you now spend on interest charges.

❑ Ask to have all dividends from mutual funds or stocks automatically reinvested.

❑ Contribute to an IRA.

❑ Save early. Thanks to compounding, $1,000 saved this year will have far greater value when you retire than the same $1,000 put away 10 or 20 years from now.

❑ Trim your spending.

modified, of course) so funds are not being wasted. Now, you should look beyond the basic start you have made in your employer retirement program, IRA or Keogh plan, to a more extensive form of investment.

SOUND INVESTMENT PROGRAM

In approaching your expanded program, you will continue to look for opportunities to reduce the "bite" of taxation by using the tax-efficient approach, where possible.

There are other important factors to look for:

Prime quality investments. Whether it is a stock fund, a certificate of deposit, or a house, explore the alternatives carefully. Comparison shop.

Diversified portfolio. Nobody—even the very best financial planner—is smart enough to call the "shots" right all the time. Experts agree on one thing: the best way to cut your investment risks is to diversify.

Balanced portfolio. Look for greater potential growth of your investment dollars by including a balance of aggressive, conservative and liquid investment instruments in your portfolio.

Minimum administrative costs. "Loads," fees and commissions can cut your investment profits excessively. So, look for "no load," minimum cost investments and avoid "turning over" your investments more often than necessary.

Consistency of contributions. As we stated earlier, consistency is an important factor in building a substantial investment fund over the years. This approach has the added advantage of letting you "dollar average" your purchases, a process that tends to hold down the average cost of shares which continually fluctuate in price.

STAY TUNED TO THE ECONOMY

We are not suggesting you should attempt to foresee and react to every change and vagary of the economic situation. Whether the economic forecast appears to be good *or* bad for the long run, it should be given major consideration in your investment planning.

In applying these investment principles, there are in general two different approaches to take:

- ❏ Do it yourself.
- ❏ Use a financial planner.

THE DO-IT-YOURSELF APPROACH

The pointers in this section will be helpful even if you decide to work with a financial planner.

The first step is to do some further study of the investment business generally. Do some reading in the field. Your library is packed with books and periodicals providing sound advice on the subject of investment practices.

Subscribe to one of the major investment-type publications. It will keep you apprised of changes, trends and prospects in the market.

Take courses on the subject of investing at one of your local colleges.

Select a "family" of funds with a proven track record. Such families include among their offerings a wide variety of mutual stock and bond funds. One big advantage of working with a "family" is that you get the privilege of moving your investments from one type of fund to another quite freely, often without a special charge for the transaction. This is an important, cost-saving factor when you need to switch from more aggressive funds to more conservative ones because of a change in the economic climate.

Getting the background information you want on these fund families is not difficult. Just look through a current investment periodical. Find the names and the toll-free phone numbers of the most prominent families and call them. Ask them to send you information brochures including details on the performance of their funds.

After you receive this literature, do a thorough "comparison check" of the various families you are considering. Also check the performance record of these funds as shown in frequent research studies, published regularly in the popular financial monthlies. Then, and only then, make a selection of a family to work with.

BALANCING YOUR PORTFOLIO

Selecting the balance you want in your portfolio is another step. In approaching this matter you should first consider your attitude toward investment "risk." If you invest in stocks and bonds, you are going to have to face the prospect of market "downs" as well as market "ups." The fact is, you can not avoid all risks just by investing conservatively. As an example, a guaranteed savings account will only earn you about 3% on your savings, which you'll have to pay taxes. Inflation in 1998 was approximately 1.5%.

Also, we should mention here the several additional types of mutual funds that should be given consideration at this stage of your planning. Previously we described money market funds, certificates of deposit, bonds and bond funds, and balanced funds. There are also:

Aggressive Growth and Long Term Growth Funds. These mutual stock funds aim at maximum growth in stock value and capital gains, while providing dividend income. However, they involve substantial risks because their aggressive investment policy, and their share prices may fluctuate widely.

Index Trust. The difficulty of beating the Dow and other market averages has been shown by numerous studies. So the index trust or index mutual stock fund was created. The list of stocks held by such funds is set up to match those

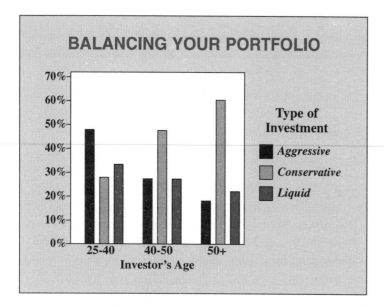

BALANCING YOUR PORTFOLIO

Type of Investment
- Aggressive
- Conservative
- Liquid

Investor's Age: 25-40, 40-50, 50+

included in one of the popular stock indexes (for example, the Standard and Poor's Index). As a result, the share price of the index trust closely follows the downs and ups of the market. Since the overall trend of stock market prices over the long run has been up, this characteristic should be advantageous in the long run.

The purpose of your "balancing" plan is to set up a portfolio of stocks that will give you, to some extent, the growth potential of aggressive mutual stock funds while retaining a measure of security against market downturns. This is accomplished through the investment of a portion

of your savings in aggressive funds, a portion in conservative funds and liquid investments.

The major fund families promote this approach to investment planning, and you will find recommendations in their brochure you can refer to in developing your own basic plan. The chart to the left also may be helpful. It is a rough summary of the recommendations of a selected group of financial planners as published recently.

You can see that the planners' recommendations became more and more weighted toward conservative investments as the investors get older and the need for security of savings becomes greater. Of course, the long term health of the economy as forecast by the financial community should also be given serious consideration.

TAKING ACTION

Actually setting up your investment program is the final action to take in getting started. Review the stocks available from the family of funds you intend to work with and make a preliminary selection. Then contact the fund family, discuss your plans for "balancing" your investment program, the tentative fund selections you have made, and get the counsel of the fund representative.

PLAN FOR RETIREMENT NOW

Advance planning for retirement should begin in your 40's, certainly no later than your early to mid-50's.

Now, more than ever before, careful financial planning is necessary to acquire the assets needed to assure a comfortable and happy retirement. This can't be put off until you are 60 or over.

Generally, a combined pension program and Social Security will yield about 60% of your pre-retirement income. You may be able to live on less after you retire, but you probably will need a supplementary income to avoid a lowered standard of living.

In your 40's and 50's, concentrate on financing retirement years. In your 50's, begin giving more serious thought to what you want in retirement, how you would like to spend your time, where you will live and what adjustments you might have to make. You should think in specific ways about retirement—and if you are married, the planning should be done jointly. In your 50's, you should have a good idea of what you're going to do in your retirement.

In your early 60's, you must begin thinking about when you will retire—at 65? Earlier, with reduced benefits? Or later?

REVIEW

Let's look at the major points we have made...

FIRST, we emphasized the need for establishing a sound financial base:

❑ An adequate working fund whose purpose is to provide money for day-to-day living and help minimize resort to debt.

❑ A "life insurance" plan that provides adequate protection at a competitive cost—particularly during early family years.

SECOND, we called attention to the need for starting a beginning savings and investment program as early in your career as possible:

❑ Consistent contributions of even modest amounts to such a program build up to significant levels over the years because of the magical effect of "compound interest."

❑ The use of employer retirement programs, IRA's and Keogh accounts for such initial investments helps to keep them as tax-free as possible and thus helps maximize their growth and appreciation.

If you have gone this far in your financial planning, you have taken a giant step toward future financial security.

THIRD, we covered the factors involved in the development of a "full blown" investment program, pointing out that it should:

❑ Be based on a thorough understanding of the characteristics of a sound program (i.e., need for diversification, balance, etc.).

❑ Involve thoughtful application of these principles whether you "do it yourself" or with a reliable financial planner.

FINANCING YOUR RETIREMENT?

QUICK FINANCIAL OVERVIEW

The first step in financial planning is to figure out where you stand today.

Take a few moments to fill out this worksheet. Don't spend a lot of time digging through records or being exact. Just make your best estimate for each category. You will want to do a more careful analysis later (see the worksheets on pages 25 and 26). You may be surprised at your financial status. This will give you a basis for your financial and retirement planning.

Monthly Income

Monthly wages; salary	$_____
Dividends/interest	$_____
Other	$_____
TOTAL MONTHLY INCOME	$_____

Monthly Expenses

Mortgage/rent	$_____
Transportation	$_____
Food	$_____
Education	$_____
Child Care	$_____
Entertainment/recreation	$_____
Loans (car/credit card, etc.)	$_____
Utilities (gas, phone, electricity, water, etc.)	$_____
Miscellaneous (clothes, insurance, medical, etc.)	$_____
TOTAL MONTHLY EXPENSES	$_____

	Monthly Income	$_____
minus	**Monthly Expenses**	- $_____
plus	**Savings and Investments**	+ $_____
equals	**TOTAL DISCRETIONARY CASH**	= $_____

RETIREMENT EXPENSE WORKSHEET

Step 1: Using this worksheet, record everything you spend for one month. If you have some expenses that don't fit any category, include them at the bottom.

Step 2: To determine your yearly expenses, multiply your monthly expenses by 12.

Step 3: To determine your projected yearly retirement expenses, multiply your yearly expenses by .80. The result is an approximation of how much you'll need per year during retirement, not factoring in inflation.

Housing (rent or mortgage, property/real estate taxes, household maintenance)	$_____
Essentials (food, clothing, medical and dental bills)	$_____
Taxes (income, property and Social Security)	$_____
Utilities (gas, electric, telephone)	$_____
Transportation (car loans, gas, car maintenance, plane, train, bus and taxi fares)	$_____
Leisure (vacation home mortgage, entertainment, travel, club dues)	$_____
Loan and installment payments (bank, auto, home equity loans, credit card debt)	$_____
Insurance (health, auto, homeowner, life, long-term care)	$_____
Gifts, charitable contributions	$_____
Investments	$_____
Total Monthly Expenses	$_____
multiply by 12 **Total Yearly Expenses**	$_____
multiply by .80 **TOTAL YEARLY RETIREMENT EXPENSES**	$_____

CASH FLOW WORKSHEET

Date: _____

INCOME LAST YEAR		IN RETIREMENT
Husband's wages or salary	$_____	$_____
Wife's wages or salary	$_____	$_____
Dividends and interest	$_____	$_____
Child support/alimony	$_____	$_____
Annuities, pensions, Social Security	$_____	$_____
Rents, royalties, fees	$_____	$_____
Other_____	$_____	$_____
TOTAL INCOME	$_____	$_____

TAXES		
Income taxes	$_____	$_____
Social Security contributions	$_____	$_____
Property taxes	$_____	$_____
TOTAL TAXES	$_____	$_____

LIVING EXPENSES		
Rent or mortgage payments	$_____	$_____
Food	$_____	$_____
Clothing	$_____	$_____
Utilities	$_____	$_____
Meals out	$_____	$_____
Furniture and other durable goods	$_____	$_____
Recreation, entertainment, vacations	$_____	$_____
Gasoline	$_____	$_____
Car payments	$_____	$_____
Financial and legal services	$_____	$_____
Doctor bills	$_____	$_____
Interest	$_____	$_____
Household maintenance	$_____	$_____
Car repairs	$_____	$_____
Tuition/day care	$_____	$_____
Life and disability insurance premiums	$_____	$_____
Grooming (i.e. laundry, cleaning)	$_____	$_____
Medications	$_____	$_____
Auto insurance premiums	$_____	$_____
Health insurance premiums	$_____	$_____
Other (i.e. gifts) _____	$_____	$_____
TOTAL ANNUAL LIVING EXPENSES	$_____	$_____

FUNDS AVAILABLE FOR **SAVINGS AND INVESTMENTS**	$_____	$_____

(total income minus taxes and living expenses)

NET WORTH WORKSHEET

Date: _____

Property Assets *

Residence	$_____
Vacation home	$_____
Furnishings	$_____
Jewelry/Art	$_____
Automobiles	$_____
Other	$_____

Equity Assets *

Real estate	$_____
Stocks	$_____
Mutual funds	$_____
Variable annuity	$_____
Business equity	$_____
Other	$_____

Cash Reserve Assets *

Checking account	$_____
Savings account	$_____
Credit union	$_____
CDs	$_____
Other	$_____

Fixed Assets *

Government bonds	$_____
Municipal bonds	$_____
Corporate bonds	$_____
Fixed annuities	$_____
Other	$_____
TOTAL ASSETS	$_____

Liabilities **

Home mortgage	$_____
Other mortgage	$_____
Bank loans	$_____
Auto loans	$_____
Personal loans	$_____
Credit card debt	$_____
Other	$_____

TOTAL LIABILITIES	$_____

TOTAL ASSETS	$_____
minus	
TOTAL LIABILITIES	- $_____
equals	
YOUR NET WORTH **	= $_____

This is your personal financial overview. You may be surprised at your net worth, especially if your home has appreciated significantly in value or if you have significant loans or credit card debt. Your cash flow and your net worth will provide the starting point for your financial future. By managing your cash flow, you can build your net worth and turn your dreams into realities.

* For calculation of your assets, use current value not the original purchase price.

** Amounts due (not monthly installments but total balances) in accounts with credit card and gasoline companies, department stores and other retailers, and to anyone else to whom you owe money. This is an important total to know and to review periodically; many who run into credit problems do so because they have lost track of how much they owe overall—it's too easy to charge.

*** To compute your net worth, total your liabilities and deduct this amount from your total assets (if the amount is larger, you're facing trouble). The result is your net worth. After you've done this one, subsequent surveys will be easier; you will have basic figures that will only need reviewing and adjusting. A 20% increase in net worth annually is considered ideal—but don't really expect such a gain until later years.

A FINANCIAL PLANNING CHECKLIST

How prepared are you?

Have you:

1. Put all your vital financial papers in one place; told someone else where they are; made copies of them?

Yes ☐   No ☐

2. Figured your retirement expenses, keeping inflation in mind; identified financial assets and projected their growth before retirement?

Yes ☐   No ☐

3. Talked over retirement finances with your spouse or, if you are single, with someone close to you?

Yes ☐   No ☐

4. Figured what survivor's benefits you or your spouse would receive if either one of you died?

Yes ☐   No ☐

5. Obtained investment and savings information; planned for improving your approach to savings and investment for further investigation?

Yes ☐   No ☐

If you checked any NO's—you know where you need to do some work.

YOU'LL NEED 60-75% OF YOUR PRESENT INCOME TO MAINTAIN YOUR PRESENT LIVING STANDARD IN RETIREMENT.

SOCIAL SECURITY

Social Security is America's most important financial program. Millions count on it for their survival. In fact, some 44 million checks go out each month. Social Security is essentially a family program that offers these major benefits:

- ❑ Disability Benefits
- ❑ Survivor Benefits
- ❑ Retirement Benefits
- ❑ Medicare Benefits

Benefits can also be paid to dependents of retired, disabled, or deceased workers (refer to Dependent Benefits Chart, page 33). Each of the major benefits will be discussed in more detail later. Social Security acts as a kind of insurance at important junctures in your family's life: retirement, disability, and death.

BECOMING INSURED

For any benefits to be paid, the worker must have worked long enough and sometimes recently enough to qualify. Work performed under Social Security earns "quarters of coverage" (or credits). Four credits can be earned in a calendar year. Before 1978, a worker had to actually earn $50 or more during a calendar quarter to earn a credit.

Beginning in 1978, yearly credits are determined by dividing the total covered earnings by a yearly increment. These increments increase every year. In 2000 one credit is earned for each $780; therefore, $3,120 will earn the four credit maximum.

The number of credits needed depends on the type of benefit involved. As a "rule of thumb," one credit is needed for each year that elapses after age 21 up to the year of age 62, death, or disability. It does not matter when the credits are earned. Disability benefits require the worker not only to be "fully insured" but also have recent work. Some survivor benefits can be paid if the worker is not "fully insured," but has earned credits in six of the thirteen calendar quarters prior to death. By doing so, the worker is considered to be "currently insured." This is especially helpful when young workers die leaving dependent children and widows/ers or former widows/ers caring for those children.

Some people think that their Social Security benefits will be based on the number of credits they have. This is not true. The dollar amount of any benefits paid has nothing to do with the number of credits you have. You either qualify or do not qualify for benefits based on credits. The calculation of the benefit amount will be discussed later.

IF RETIREMENT IS FAR AWAY

The Social Security Administration has been keeping records of your earnings throughout your working life. Are those records accurate and up-to-date? Imagine filing for your benefits and finding yourself shortchanged or delayed because of errors made years ago.

Check Your Record: In October 1999, Social Security began mailing annual statements to every worker age 25 or older. Your statement should be received in the third month prior to your month of birth. For example, if you were born in the month of June, you should receive your annual statement in the month of March. If you do not receive an annual statement, call Social Security 800-772-1213 or www.ssa.gov.

Review your statement carefully and report any errors *immediately* to the Social Security office nearest you. You can do this by telephone. Note the date, time, and name of the person you spoke with in your own records.

Check for Overpayments: You may also find an employer did not stop collecting Social Security taxes after reaching the maximum taxable amount in a given year or you worked for more than one employer and your total wages exceeded the maximum. In this event you can receive a refund or a credit against your federal income tax. Request it on your income tax return.

RETIREMENT BENEFITS

Very few people find their Social Security checks sufficient to cover their expenses. We suggest you find out what you can expect from Social Security and how it will fit into your retirement plans. Your Social Security retirement benefits will be based on your lifetime earnings. Many people think that only the last five years are used to calculate benefits, nothing could be further from the truth. Everyone retiring in the future (born in 1929 and later) will have 35 years of earnings averaged together to determine their benefit computation.

For an explanation of how retirement benefits are figured, ask Social Security for the fact sheet, *How Your Retirement Benefit is Figured.*

EARLY VS. LATE RETIREMENT

As you look ahead to retirement, you may be thinking "...the earlier the better." But if Social Security is going to be your *only* source of income, "the later, the better" applies.

Early retirement decreases your retirement benefits. If you take your benefits before full retirement age (FRA), they are permanently reduced. The amount of the reduction depends on the number of months you elect benefits prior to full retirement age; however in term of dollars

AGE TO RECEIVE FULL SOCIAL SECURITY BENEFITS

Year of Birth	Full Retirement Age*
1937 or earlier	65
1938	65 and 2 months
1939	65 and 4 months
1940	65 and 6 months
1941	65 and 8 months
1942	65 and 10 months
1943-1954	66
1955	66 and 2 months
1956	66 and 4 months
1957	66 and 6 months
1958	66 and 8 months
1959	66 and 10 months
1960 and later	67

* If you take monthly benefits before full retirement age your benefits are reduced.

received from Social Security, a worker retiring at 62, is usually about 12 years ahead because of the additional checks received between age 62 and full retirement age.

If you decide to retire before full retirement age, or you have very low earnings, you should consider filing early. For a more detailed explanation of the best time to contact Social Security to avoid possible loss of benefits, refer to the section entitled, "When to Contact Social Security" (page 35).

If you wait to retire after age 65, your benefit is increased for each year you continue working after age 65 (delayed retirement credits). The percentage of these delayed credits increases over time and will reach 8% by the year 2009.

As a quick check on how much you can look forward to at full retirement age, consider what

SPECIAL NOTE: Even if you file for reduced benefits, at full retirement age you will be given credit for any months you did not receive a full check because of work. This is commonly referred to by Social Security as an automatic adjustment of your reduction factor.

WHAT YOU PAY FOR SOCIAL SECURITY & MEDICARE
(Worker Amount Matched by Employer)

Year	% Tax Rate	Maximum Taxable Wage Base	Employee Maximum Tax
1970	4.80	7,800	374.40
1980	6.13	25,900	1,587.67
1990	7.65	51,000	3,924.45
1995	7.65	61,200	4,681.80
1997	7.65	65,400	5,003.10
1998	7.65	68,400	5,232.60
1999	7.65	72,600	5,553.90
2000	7.65	76,200	5,829.30

Amount for each year is based on increases in average earnings of all employees in the country.

percentage of your income will be replaced by your retirement benefits. If your lifetime earnings were average, you can expect to receive a benefit of about $11,844 a year. The average eligible couple receives about $17,766 a year (both worker and spouse at full retirement age).

If you have always paid the maximum in Social Security deductions, you can count on a benefit of about 24% of that amount. In 1999 the maximum earnings subject to Social Security taxes were $72,600 generating $17,196 a year in retirement benefits. As long as you work you will pay FICA taxes.

HUSBANDS AND WIVES

Both husband and wife are eligible to receive Social Security benefits, even if only one has earned enough credits. The worker who qualifies will receive at retirement his or her own benefits. The "non-qualified" spouse (the spouse who has not worked enough to qualify) will receive a benefit equal to a percentage of the worker's benefit. Usually the "non-qualified" spouse must be age 62 to receive this spousal benefit.

If both husband and wife qualify on their own for Social Security, both will receive their own benefits. In those instances where one spouse's benefit is less than half of the other's, the lesser-

paid spouse will usually receive his or her own benefit *plus* a spousal benefit.

The spousal benefit provisions in no way reduce the worker's benefits. Similarly, spousal benefits payable to the current spouse are not affected by any benefits being paid to a former spouse.

Important to note is that though a spouse may be eligible for benefits at age 62 *without* having worked, the same is not true for disability benefits. You must have worked *and* meet certain other conditions to receive disability benefits. There is no disability spouses benefits.

SOCIAL SECURITY TABLES

Remember, the maximum amount of earnings covered by Social Security was lower in past years than it is now. Those years of lower limits must be counted in with the higher ones of recent years to figure your average earnings, and the amount of your monthly retirement check.

The Social Security tables are based on assumptions for people attaining age 65 in 2000 who earned the salaries shown in 1999—assuming they had worked steadily in covered employment since age 22.

Except for persons who have always paid the maximum, the amount payable in any particular case could vary greatly from those illustrated.

ESTIMATED MONTHLY AND FIRST-YEAR SOCIAL SECURITY INCOME PAYABLE AS OF JANUARY 2000 TO A 65-YEAR-OLD PERSON

[1] Salary in Year Before Retirement	[2] Monthly	[3] First Year Social Security Income	[4] Approximate Replacement Ratio
$10,000	$524	$6,228	63%
20,000	769	9,228	46%
30,000	1,014	12,168	41%
40,000	1,224	14,688	37%
50,000	1,307	15,684	34%
60,000	1,376	16,512	28%
72,600	1,433	17,196	24%

Notes to chart: Because $72,600 was the maximum taxable 1999 Social Security wage base, Social Security will, of course, replace an increasingly smaller portion of earnings that exceed it.

Maximum benefits for a worker attaining age 65 in 2000 is $1,433 per month—an increase of $60 per month over 1999. Replacement rate numbers are only tentative until prior year average wages are determined.

These figures assume you have worked regularly and received yearly wage increases.

Note: *For a couple* the average Social Security benefit is about $17,766 a year (both worker and spouse at full retirement age).

In fact, persons spending much of their careers either in *non-covered* employment or *outside* the work force altogether, might receive less payment.

The tables also assume that the worker does not qualify for a "non covered" pension.

Anyone who does qualify for a pension based on work that was not covered for Social Security taxes may not have the same computation method. Social Security can provide a fact sheet *A Pension From Work Not Covered By Social Security* that explains this in detail.

AUTOMATIC SOCIAL SECURITY COST-OF-LIVING ADJUSTMENTS

Once you are on the Social Security rolls, your checks will increase automatically to keep pace with increases in the cost of living.

In addition, additional earnings after initial entitlement can be considered in a recalculation of your rate.

SURVIVOR BENEFITS

Survivor benefits to dependent children and young widows/ers can be paid, based on "fully or currently" insured status. The amount of benefits payable to any survivor is determined by the covered earnings of the deceased worker.

A rate is calculated as if the worker was age 62 in the year of death and a primary insurance amount (PIA) is established. Each dependent is entitled to a percentage of the PIA; however, there is a maximum amount payable. (Refer to the Chart on page 33, for more specific information.)

A one-time lump-sum death payment of $255 is payable to either a widow/er entitled to benefits, a widow/er not entitled to monthly benefits, or to children entitled to benefits.

Benefits due divorced spouses are not considered in the family maximum. In other words, the divorced spouse takes nothing away from the current spouse or widow and vice versa.

WIDOWS AND WIDOWERS

Today, in many families both spouses have worked and paid Social Security. Most qualify for retirement as early as age 62. Some may have been widowed and received Social Security benefits prior to age 62 as a widow/er benefit. This person at reaching the age of 62 should check with Social Security and find out the dollar amount of a retirement check they could receive if they filed for benefits based on their own work record. If the widow/er qualified for a higher rate, he or she could switch to his or her own record.

Before deciding to switch, we recommend that you find out what the dollar amount of your own retirement benefits would be at 62, at full retirement age, and at age 70. Most widows/ers are told the rates for age 62 and age 65; however most Social Security employees fail to tell you what the rate would be if you wait until age 70. At age 70, delayed retirement credits can be added to your own basic retirement benefit and will significantly increase the total retirement check. We have seen many widows/ers who were told that there was no need to file a claim on their own work because the widows/ers rate was higher. They were not advised that if they waited until age 70 to file on their own work record, their own retirement check amount would exceed the widow/er rate.

OTHER RESOURCES

Social Security Administration provides pamphlets. Call toll-free **1 (800) 772-1213** to request copies or www.ssa.gov.

❑ A Pension From Work Not Covered by Social Security
❑ Agricultural Workers
❑ Financing Social Security
❑ Government Pension Offset
❑ Help For Low Income Medicare Beneficiaries
❑ Household Workers
❑ How Work Affects Your Social Security Benefits
❑ How Your Retirement Benefit is Figured
❑ Military Service and Social Security
❑ Reporting Farm Income
❑ Reviewing Your Disability
❑ Social Security and Your Right to Representation
❑ Special Wage Payments After Retirement
❑ The Appeals Process
❑ When You Retire From Your Own Business What Social Security Needs to Know

3 WAYS TO INSURE A SOUND FINANCIAL RETIREMENT

SOCIAL SECURITY BENEFITS FOR DEPENDENTS

Dependent is age...	and...	then these benefits may be payable...	at the following % of PIA...
0-19	a child of a deceased or entitled worker*	minor child or student benefits	50% (worker alive) 75% (worker deceased)
18 and older	disabled before age 22 and parent is either deceased or entitled	disabled adult child benefits	50% (worker alive) 75% (worker deceased)
up to FRA**	a young widow/er or divorced widow/er with child in care under age 16	mother/father benefits	75%
50-60	a disabled widow/er or a surviving divorced widow/er	disabled widow/er benefits	71.5%
60+	a widow/er, surviving divorced spouse	widow/er's benefit	varies from 71.5% to 100% depending on age at entitlement
62+	1) currently married to entitled worker	spouse benefits	varies from 37.5% to 50% depending on age at entitlement
	2) divorces after 10 years of marriage to entitled worker	divorced spouse benefits	
	3) divorced after 10 years of marriage to an age 62 worker not entitled but insured	independently entitled divorced spouse benefits	
	4) surviving parent	parent's benefits	82.5% if one 75% each if two

This table assumes that the individual meets all of the dependency rules
* See Chapter 15 for information for grandchildren   **Full Retirement Age

DISABILITY BENEFITS

The risk of disability hangs over all of us. A loss of earnings due to severe injury or illness can affect a family more than the retirement or death of the breadwinner.

Social Security provides basic protection against disability for most Americans and their families. Currently, about 4.8 million adults receive disability checks.

There is a five-month waiting period before disability payments can begin. This period begins with the first full month of disability and ends five months later. *No payment is made for that period.*

As mentioned earlier, under Social Security a disabled worker must be fully insured and have recent work in order to be qualified. During the ten-year period just before becoming disabled, the worker must have five years of credits (20). **Workers becoming disabled prior to age 31 need fewer credits.** Workers who are statutorily blind must only be "fully insured."

It is very important for a worker to understand the "recent work" requirement, particularly persons opting for "early out" retirements with their company. If you plan on retiring prior to age 56 you should consider working at another job and acquiring four credits per year *through the year* you attain age 56. By doing so, you will continue to have enough recent work to qualify you for disability until you reach age 62.

Dependents of disabled workers can also receive benefits within the family maximum payable.

MEDICARE BENEFITS

Medicare is a national health insurance program for people who are age 65; have been receiving Social Security disability benefits for 24 months; or have End Stage Renal Disease. It is administered by the Social Security Administration. The Health Care Finance Administration is responsible for processing reimbursements for covered medical services. **Whether or not you apply for Social Security at age 65, you should apply at least three months in advance of your 65th birthday to be covered by Medicare**. (See Chapter 7)

WORK AND SOCIAL SECURITY

With the exception of a disabled worker or an adult disabled child, *all* Social Security beneficiaries are subject to an earnings test up until age 70. Social Security sets a yearly limit on the amount of earnings you can have before withholding some of your benefits. These limits increase every year.

If you are under age 65 in 2000 the limit is $10,080. The limit is $17,000 for persons age 65

EARNINGS LIMIT AGE 65 - 69

2000	$17,000
2001	$25,000
2002	$30,000

Note: The annual exempt amount after 2002 will be indexed to growth in wages.

SOCIAL SECURITY PAYMENT DATES

New beneficiaries will receive monthly checks or deposits based on day of birth:

1-10	2nd Wednesday of the month
11-20	3rd Wednesday of the month
21-31	4th Wednesday of the month

HOW TO CONTACT SOCIAL SECURITY

800-772-1213
or
www.ssa.gov

and older. There is no limit once you are age 70. In fact, earnings during the month you turn 70 and thereafter, do not count toward the annual limit. Earnings include only income from work or from self-employment. Investment income (dividends, real estate, rentals, and return on capital) is *not* counted as earnings. Neither are pensions.

If you do earn more than the yearly limit, you lose some of your Social Security benefits. One dollar is withheld for every two dollars above the limit for all persons younger than age 65. One dollar for every *three* is withheld for persons 65 through 69. This "one for three" rule is significant. Many people could receive some Social Security benefits for the year even while working full time.

There is a special rule that can apply to your initial year of retirement. It is called the "grace year" rule, meaning that workers are allowed a monthly earning limit for each month in that year. The monthly limit is simply the annual limit divided by twelve. This special rule usually applies only for one year, but helps those persons who have high earnings in the months prior to retirement.

Ask Social Security for the fact sheet, *How Work Affects Your Social Security Benefits.*

WHEN TO CONTACT

Survivors of deceased workers should contact Social Security as soon as possible after the death of the worker. Disabled workers should contact Social Security as soon as their physician advises that their medical condition is expected to last at least twelve months.

Effective January 1991, retirement applications can no longer be retroactive. Prior to 1991, if there were any advantages to having your retirement claim effective earlier than the month you filed, Social Security would allow the claim to be effective as early as six months before your application date. Since this can no longer be done, we recommend that persons age 62 should:

❏ Contact Social Security three months prior to age 62, if you have retired or are planning to retire at age 62

OR

❏ Contact Social Security every January (even if working full time). Provide them with an estimate of your current year earnings, and ask them to determine the dollar amount of any benefits you might be eligible for if you filed a formal claim. Remember to tell Social Security if there are any dependents who will also be eligible for benefits on your record.

BENEFITS MAY BE TAXABLE

Up to one-half of your benefits may be subject to the Federal income tax for any year in which your adjusted gross income plus non-taxable interest income and one-half of your Social Security benefits exceed a base amount of $25,000 for an individual, $32,000 for a couple, and zero for a couple filing separately. Should your adjusted gross income exceed $34,000 for an individual or $44,000 for a couple, 85% of excess benefits are taxable.

SUPPLEMENTAL SECURITY INCOME

People in financial need who are 65 or older or people of any age who are blind or disabled may be eligible for a monthly cash payment from the Federal government. These payments are called supplemental security income (SSI).

People may be eligible for payments if they have little or no regular cash income and don't own much in the way of assets that can be turned into cash. The Social Security Administration operates the program but SSI is not the same as Social Security. Social Security funds are not used to make SSI payments. Applications for SSI are made at the Social Security office. In most states, Medicaid is provided for anyone eligible for SSI.

SOCIAL SECURITY: THEN AND NOW

When the Social Security Act was passed the average American died at 63. Most people wouldn't live to collect Social Security and those who did wouldn't collect it for long.

Today the average American will live to about 75, actually 72 for men and 79 for women.

When Social Security was launched in 1937, more than 40 contributors supported each recipient. Until 1949, the maximum contribution was $30 per year. A lot has changed since then. Longevity has increased. Social Security has expanded to include more benefits and more recipients.

By 1999 there were just three contributors to pay for each recipient and the cap on contributions was $5553.90. About a third of the workforce now pays more to Social Security than to the IRS.

PLANNING YOUR ESTATE

If a fire destroys your home, how much will you lose? If you have fire insurance, you may have the value of the house covered to the extent that you can have it replaced for no additional expense. **What will happen in the event of your death?** Will your estate be turned over to your family without loss? Carelessness in making plans for your estate increase the chances that what you have accumulated over the years may be disposed of in ways you would not approve.

Before skipping to the next chapter thinking that you don't have an estate, and that everything will be left to your spouse, let's define what is an "estate." You may not have much to leave when you die, but the U.S. government may have a less modest opinion of what you are leaving. As of 2000, the federal government imposes a tax on estates over $675,000, this will be increased by stages to $1 million in 2006. It then will be indexed for inflation Family farms and family businesses will be eligible for an exemption of $1.3 million in 1998. Some states have their own inheritance or estate taxes.

An individual's estate consists of the many valuable assets accumulated during the lifetime. These include: life insurance, accounts in banks and credit unions, social security, stocks, bonds, pension and profit-sharing plans, real estate, stock options, business and professional interests, investments, employee fringe benefits, etc.

For the purpose of taxation the "gross estate" is composed of all assets an individual owns at the time of death, plus any property at the time of death, and gifts made in contemplation of death. "Taxable estate" is the gross estate, less liabilities. Don't assume that your spouse will automatically receive your property. If there is no will, the estate may be disposed of according to the laws of descent of the state where the property is located. Even if you have all your property jointly owned, the absence of a will may cause your spouse to wait several months before gaining possession of the property.

OWNING PROPERTY

Check with your attorney: which of the four types of property ownership best suits your needs?
Joint Tenancy with Right of Survivorship: Two or more people hold property jointly and one person dies—the other or others automatically receive the dead person's interest.
Tenancy by the Entirety: Limited to husbands and wives. Both spouses have to agree as to disposal of the property.
Tenancy in Common: When two or more people hold shares in property and one dies, his or her shares passes to that person's heirs.
Community Property: Eight states have laws holding that *all* property acquired during marriage is owned by each spouse equally.

RELUCTANCE TO MAKE A WILL

Many people have not made a will. Reasons may be: superstition and procrastination. Some feel that thinking about a will may hasten the moment when it can be needed. If we don't notice approaching age or think about mortality, maybe it won't notice us. It's unpleasant to think about such a "grim" subject. "It will be easier to think about it tomorrow!"

WHY MAKE A WILL?

A will is a written instrument executed with the formalities prescribed by law, whereby a person directs the disposition of his or her property after death.

If you make a will, your property will go to the person(s) named and in the amounts you specify. If you fail to make a will, the law arbitrarily distributes your property according to prevailing regulations.

WHEN YOU DON'T HAVE A WILL...

Making a will may save money by reducing expenses. If you do not have a will: your heirs will not be able to sell, distribute, or handle property without the expense of asking a court for authority; your estate or inheritance taxes may be higher than they need legally be; the person who administers your estate will have to post a bond; your property may be dealt with, your business operated or concluded, and your real estate sold with losses.

If you make a will, you can name the person you wish to handle your estate. Where no will exists, the matter of who will administer the estate can be the occasion for painful disputes and needless expense. When an executor is named, he must post a bond, the premium for which must be taken from the estate. (A bond can be dispensed with *if* the will so provides.) This administrator can only liquidate your assets, pay your debts, and distribute the remainder of your property. Executors have limited authority to deal with real property, business, or other property.

DISPOSITION OF ESTATES

You can use a will to make outright disposition of your assets. You can also make outright gifts of parcels of your estate during your lifetime. You can create a "trust" by transferring your estate, or part of it, to a trustee. You may live off the income it provides during your lifetime, with the principal being disposed of later. You can also set up a "testamentary trust" which assures income for your spouse or dependents. This type of arrangement protects them against their own inexperience in the management of the estate.

KEEPING WILLS UP TO DATE

Wills which were valid years ago should be reviewed periodically. Circumstances may have changed so that particulars referred to in the will no longer exist, or things exist which the original will did not cover.

The following changes should cause you to look *again* at the condition of your will:

❑ Change of mind about beneficiaries
❑ Executor dies
❑ Change in family situation
❑ Change in financial situation
❑ Change in the nature of assets
❑ Change in the needs of the beneficiaries
❑ Change of residence, state or country

CONSIDER TRUSTS

Trusts may be an ideal method to handle some of your assets. Basically, a trust is a plan whereby a trustee holds money that you have transferred, and manages it according to a written trust agreement.

Trusts may be living or testamentary; revocable or irrevocable. Example: you wish to transfer twenty thousand dollars to a trust for your grandchildren's education while you're alive—a living trust. If the trust was created by your will, it's testamentary.

A revocable trust can be canceled by the person who establishes it; an irrevocable trust cannot be terminated.

Trusts cost money—check with your attorney or the trust officer of your bank.

Trusts have advantages under certain conditions. They could save money and time. Be informed—read books and articles on trusts. Check with your library and consult your attorney.

TO AVOID PROBLEMS LATER YOU'LL NEED:

A Power of Attorney	There may be an occasion when you could not act on your own behalf in certain legal matters. You may grant someone you trust your "Power of Attorney" to act for you. You do this by signing a notarized document specifying the details of what matter the "Power of Attorney" should represent you in and for what period of time the document is effective.
A Durable Power of Attorney for Health Care	A Durable Power of Attorney for Health Care makes clear your wishes about your future medical care. It tells doctors and hospital employees whether you want to be kept alive if you're in a coma or suffering a terminal illness beyond all reasonable hope of recovery. It names someone you trust to carry out your wishes. You can specify what should be done after consultation with family members, medical doctors and your Minister, Priest or Rabbi. State laws differ—check with an attorney or your local Office of Aging.
To Update or Make a Will	There may be changes in your situation, be sure your will reflects your wishes.
To Consider Setting Up a Trust	It avoids probate and allows a trustee to manage your assets if you become incompetent.

WILL FACT SHEET

Name:_____ Date this form completed:_____

Telephone number at home:_____ at work:_____

Street address:_____

City:_____ County:_____ State:_____ Zip code:_____

	YOURSELF	**YOUR SPOUSE**

Name:_____

Social Security number:_____

Occupation:_____

Date and place of birth:_____

Driver's license number:_____

Military service:_____

Date/place of marriage:_____

Date of divorce:_____

Death of spouse:_____

CHILDREN

Name (also of spouse):_____ Date and place of birth:_____

Telephone number at home:_____ at work:_____

Street address:_____ City:_____ State:_____ Zip code:_____

Name (also of spouse):_____ Date and place of birth:_____

Telephone number at home:_____ at work:_____

Street address:_____ City:_____ State:_____ Zip code:_____

Name (also of spouse):_____ Date and place of birth:_____

Telephone number at home:_____ at work:_____

Street address:_____ City:_____ State:_____ Zip code:_____

BENEFIT PLANS

Pension plan:_____ Value (if known): $ _____

Thrift plan: _____ Value (if known): $ _____

Profit-sharing plan:_____ Value (if known): $ _____

Other:_____ Value (if known): $ _____

Other:_____ Value (if known): $ _____

Other:_____ Value (if known): $ _____

Other:_____ Value (if known): $ _____

Other:_____ Value (if known): $ _____

HEALTH INSURANCE

Company:_____ Policy number:_____

Street address:_____ Agent: _____

City, State, Zip code: _____ Beneficiaries: _____

Telephone:_____ Location of policy:_____

Company:_____ Policy number:_____

Street address:_____ Agent: _____

City, State, Zip code:_____ Beneficiaries: _____

Telephone:_____ Location of policy:_____

HOME AND AUTO INSURANCE

Company:_____ Policy number:_____

Street address:_____ Agent: _____

City, State, Zip code:_____ Type of coverage: _____

Telephone:_____ Location of policy:_____

Company:_____ Policy number:_____

Street address:_____ Agent: _____

City, State, Zip code:_____ Type of coverage: _____

Telephone:_____ Location of policy:_____

ASSETS INVENTORY

	CURRENT VALUE	ORIGINAL COST	OWNERSHIP	LOCATION
Home:				
Business:				
Savings account:				
Checking account:				
Pensions plans:				
Household furniture:				
Stamp collection:				
Bonds:				
Trust funds:				
Stocks:				
Other:				

LIABILITY INVENTORY

Loans:_____ Amount: $ _____

Debts:_____ Amount: $ _____

Mortgages:_____ Amount: $ _____

Other:_____ Amount: $ _____

LIFE INSURANCE

Company/agent:_____ Face amount of policy:_____

Type of policy:_____ Cash surrender value:_____

Policy number:_____ Accidental death provision:_____

Telephone:_____ Beneficiaries:_____

Company/agent:_____ Face amount of policy:_____

Type of policy:_____ Cash surrender value:_____

Policy number:_____ Accidental death provision:_____

Telephone:_____ Beneficiaries:_____

LOCATION OF RECORDS, LICENSES, ETC.

Birth:_____   Deed:_____

Marriage:_____   Mortgage:_____

Adoption:_____   Title policy insurance:_____

Citizenship:_____   Title abstract:_____

Pre/postnuptial:_____   Surveys:_____

Divorce:_____   Insurance policies:_____

Discharge papers:_____   Tax receipts:_____

Building costs:_____   Leases:_____

SAFE DEPOSIT BOX

Institution where located:_____   Box number:_____

Street address:_____   Who has access:_____

City, State, Zip code:_____   Location of key:_____

Contents:_____

A list of how you would like your personal effects distributed (jewelry, art, etc.) and your burial instructions should be placed in a safe place but *not* in your safe deposit box.

PEOPLE WHO KNOW ABOUT MY AFFAIRS

Attorney:_____   Telephone number:_____

Power of attorney:_____   Telephone number:_____

Accountant:_____   Telephone number:_____

Broker:_____   Telephone number:_____

Doctor:_____   Telephone number:_____

Banker:_____   Telephone number:_____

Clergy/Rabbi:_____   Telephone number:_____

Employer/union rep.:_____   Telephone number:_____

Insurance agent:_____   Telephone number:_____

Executor of estate:_____   Telephone number:_____

HANGING ON TO YOUR MONEY

"A fool and his money ..."
"Let the buyer beware."
"There's one born every minute!"

Hanging on to your retirement money is often a difficult task, but by keeping your eyes wide open you can avoid the common pitfalls that threaten to deplete your pocketbook.

THE PURCHASER

Studies show that the typical consumer's buying habits needlessly strain the budget.

❑ Most grocery shoppers never use a list and shop in only one grocery store.

❑ Customers who charge their purchases buy three times as much as those who pay cash.

❑ Many buy nonessential items on credit for which they would not pay cash.

❑ Many people do not know how to budget their paycheck to last throughout the month.

It is estimated that as much as 20% of the average grocery bill could be saved if some simple rules were followed in the supermarket. The average family spends about 25% of its budget on food. If your income is $600 a month, your food budget could be $150. A saving of 20% would provide the same amount of food for $120. How can this be done? We thought you would never ask!

SAVING AT THE SUPERMARKET

Consider the following:

❑ Always plan your food shopping; make and use a list.

❑ *Never* shop while hungry.

❑ Avoid impulse buying.

❑ Shop at two or three different supermarkets for competitive prices. Check weekly ads.

❑ Shop only once or twice a week, and do not stay beyond a half hour. (Each minute you stay after a half hour costs you 50¢!)

❑ Avoid paying for packaging, as may be the case in some convenience foods.

❑ Consider buying the local store's brand which corresponds to the quality of nationally advertised brands. You can save up to 20%.

❑ Avoid diet foods, if possible. Buy regular foods and eat less. (However, if you are on a special diet prescribed by your doctor—salt free, low cholesterol, etc.—you should, of course, stay with what is recommended.)

❑ Learn to compare cost per unit/price.

❑ Learn to substitute fish, poultry, smaller quantities of meat for meals which rely heavily on meat. (Rice, noodles, etc. extend the meat dish.)

❑ Become familiar with grading regulations. A higher grade may refer to the *appearance* of meat, eggs, rather than to *nutritional value.*

❑ Keep a list of prices charged for similar items in the different stores you shop.

❑ Check coupon and trading stamps to see that you are not paying higher prices for items in the store to make up for "savings."

❑ Make sure "specials" are items you need.

❑ Use nonfat dry and evaporated milk and cut a third off your milk bill.

❑ Stock up on items in season and on sale.

❑ Arrive at a sensible balance between your time, your money, and your health.

CREDIT CARDS: EASY TO ABUSE

Credit cards are now easy to get, too easy perhaps. Be careful. Pay cash and stay out of trouble.The same thinking should go into a credit card transaction as goes into one involving cash. What you charge on a credit card costs you more if months drag on without full payment.

KEEP IN MIND: when you charge a purchase on a credit card and do not pay for it in full when the bill comes in, interest charges begin. **Be Careful.**

CREDIT CARD DEBT

By paying more than the minimum monthly payment, you can reduce the overall interest charged to you. If you owe $1000 on a credit card that charges 18%, paying off just an extra $10 to $30 a month shortens the payoff period **and saves you interest and money.**

MONTHLY PAYMENT	TOTAL INTEREST	TIME TO PAY OFF
$20(minimum)	$862.10	94 months
$30	$400.87	47 months
$50	$197.82	24 months

The average household credit card balance was $4,722 in 1998. The yearly interest was approximately $725 per card—bad news. The good news is that 42% of consumers are now paying their credit cards bills in full each month.

Paying off your credit card debt is the best investment you can make.

CREDIT SOLICITATIONS

For every credit offer you received a corresponding inquiry has been made into your credit report.

Under a recent revision of the Fair Credit Reporting Act, credit bureaus are required to set up toll free numbers so that consumers can call to "opt out" of preapproved credit offers.

A phone call will close your credit file for two years. Equifax 1-800-556-4711, Experian, 1-800-353-0809, Trans Union 1-800-680-7293. To close your file permanently you must fill out and send a written request form.

TELEMARKETING

Telemarketing can be a convenient way to learn about products and services and make purchases without leaving your home. If you have a telephone, chances are you've been called by a telemarketer. The Federal Trade Commission (FTC) and the State Attorney Generals have declared telemarketing fraud a key priority. Consumers be aware, many telemarketers represent honest, reputable companies, but there are those who will attempt to take your money.

The Federal Trade Commission estimates that fraudulent telemarketers swindle consumers out of more than one billion dollars each year.

STOP THE SCAMS

- ❑ Resist high pressure sales tactics. Legitimate businesses respect that you're not interested.
- ❑ If you don't want the seller to call you back, say so, if they call back, hang up. They're breaking the law.
- ❑ Take your time. Ask for written information about the subject of the call.
- ❑ Your financial investments may have consequences. Before you respond to a phone solicitation, talk to a friend, family member, or a financial advisor.
- ❑ Don't pay for prizes. Free is Free!
- ❑ Don't send cash, check or money order by courier, overnight delivery or wire to anyone who insists on immediate payment.
- ❑ Never give your credit card, bank account, or social security number to a telemarketer.
- ❑ If you suspect a scam call your State Attorney General.

CAUTION IN THE CAR LOT

Approximately 32% of all new cars are now leased. And consumer complaints regarding leasing terms have deluged the Federal Trade Commission and State Attorney Generals.

The Federal Reserve Board has responded with new rules governing car leasing effective October 1997. The rules state that key leasing conditions be disclosed in simple language, instead of being buried in the contract's fine print. The form can be obtained from the Federal Reserve Board, Publication Services, 20th and C Street NW, Washington, DC 20551 or call 202-542-3245. Ask for The Keys to Vehicle Leasing.

Although the rules are helpful you should understand the basic facts of auto leasing. It is rarely a sound financial move.

When you lease a car you spend less on a monthly basis than you would buying a car but at the end of the lease you don't own a car. Businesses use this arrangement for income tax deductions but the rest of us cannot.

For the rest of the world, there are two cheaper ways to buy a car. Buy an affordable car and keep it for at least one year after it's paid off or look for a good used car.

Car repair is another sad chapter in the life of the frustrated consumer. Experts estimate that $25 billion is spent *needlessly* each year on car repairs.

Even if you aren't a mechanic, you can: keep the water and oil clean (check both and change the latter according to the instructions in the owner's manual); keep your battery terminals clean and keep your tires inflated to the pressure recommended in your owner's manual.

Find someone you can trust who can help with the maintenance of your car. Use the services of a diagnostic clinic to obtain estimates of anticipated repairs.

Learn something about automobile maintenance and repair. Read books like Anthony Till's *What You Should Know Before You Have Your Car Repaired*, Sherbourne Press, Inc. Take a course at your adult center.

CAR LEASING CONCERNS

The following are the top 10 complaints about leases, according to a national phone survey of 6,108 first-time lease customers completed in 1996:

1. New model more expensive without added value
2. Disposition fees
3. Dealer reluctant to place lease at lowest-price finance company
4. Wear and tear charges excessive
5. Excess mileage charges excessive
6. Purchase option more expensive than expected
7. Existing lease was too long
8. Choice of lease-contract sources not provided
9. Option to re-lease same vehicle not explained
10. Existing lease too short

USED CAR PURCHASES

A car has depreciated to half of its original value after two years, but may still have three-quarters of its life left. The perils which confront the buyer in this field are so numerous that we hesitate to make recommendations. Some people trade cars when *they* begin to have trouble with them. Some people buy the cars which other people traded when they began to have trouble with them.

Check your Blue Book. Determine the kind of car you want to buy. Find the most expensive example of the model you want and have it checked by an independent mechanic. If possible, contact the former owner. Check the car's maintenance record. Shop for competitive deals, then, get the car for the best price you can obtain from the dealer. Doing business with a reputable used car dealer who has been in business for a long time and has established a record for honesty and service may be the **best** advice.

HEALTH CARE HAZARDS

Americans spend $500 million each year on vitamins, minerals, and health remedies *they don't need*. The Food and Drug Administration emphasizes that sensible eating can provide most of the nutrients the body needs, and everyday, cheaper foods may be as healthy as so-called health foods.

Americans are vulnerable to health swindles because we are health-conscious. We have come to think of science as achieving all of its goals. It must have found a remedy for our ailment.

We are exposed to articles and advertisements about health. We hear about new health practices in other countries, often different from those in our own country.

The American Medical Association suggests that you can recognize a "quack" by any of the following:

- Relies on a "special" formula or "secret" device to effect a cure.
- Implies a quick or easy cure.
- Relies heavily on testimonials from patients.
- Will not allow methods to be examined by competent medical authorities.
- Scoffs at the practice of medicine and claims that he is being persecuted by medical men.
- Claims that methods are superior to those used by medical doctors.

The American Medical Association recommends the following to protect you from fraud:

- Leave your diagnosis to your physician.
- Take medications *only* under the prescription of your physician.
- Be wary about testimonials. Even genuine cures may not be due to the causes held responsible for them. Spontaneous remission may account for relief which is supposed to have come from another source.
- Beware of "sure cures" for ailments such as arthritis, for which no known cure has been found.

- Avoid products which promise more than temporary relief for minor arthritis pains.
- Check all medications with your physician before taking them.
- Consult your pharmacist about how to take your medication, and other drug information.

STRETCHING HEALTH CARE $$$

You should not skimp on your health care but there are steps you can take to reduce health care cost. Consider the following:

- Have regular checkups; catch complaints or problems *before* they develop into chronic, life-threatening illnesses.
- Use the telephone to consult about minor health problems.
- Know which public health services are available for screening and detection of diseases.
- Find out about free clinics operated by service-oriented agencies.
- Avoid confinement in the hospital for diagnostic tests and treatment which could be given as an outpatient.
- Do not insist on a private room, unless this is important for you, or covered by your insurance.
- Investigate the possibility of having the services of a visiting nurse before going to the hospital. Room and board are cheaper at home than at the hospital, if all you need is medical attention.
- Research group purchasing plans available to unions, consumer cooperatives, and senior citizens.
- Ask your doctor to write your prescription in generic terms. This can be much cheaper than buying brand names of the same medicine.
- Compare drug prices by calling both drug stores and pharmacy services such as AARP. Ask for a senior discount.

SUCCESS: WITHOUT REALLY TRYING

Your income in retirement is less than it was before retirement. You would welcome the additional security which the provision of more income, or the protection against greater expense, would afford. Many unscrupulous operators are ready to take advantage of the vulnerable position of the aged by offering "much for little."

How can we recognize the schemes which lie in wait to steal our purse? Shakespeare obviously was not writing about the retired person's limited financial resources when he said, "He who steal my purse, steals trash …." A lot of us would like to keep our purse intact from the trash who would like to empty it for us!

The following have frequently been traps into which many individuals have fallen:

❑ **Work-at-home**—These opportunities appear in the newspaper and usually are designed to sell the products which are to be the basis of the lucrative home industry. Sometimes a registration fee is required, following which the applicant is advised that his products do not measure up to the high standards of the promoter.

   The Better Business Bureau warns against the following tactics:
   (a) Help wanted column ads with no offer of employment.
   (b) Offer of huge profits.
   (c) Emphasis on large, part-time earnings.
   (d) Use of testimonials with no way to check with the individuals.
   (e) Sell materials, kits, instructions, and equipment at high prices.
   (f) Guaranteed market.
   (g) Exaggerated demand for product.
   (h) Claim that no experience is necessary.

❑ **Purchase of franchise**—Newspaper ads used to offer great profits for little work. Exclusive territories, trained personnel to assist, and financial help is promised. Check with bank, lawyer, and Better Business Bureau before investing money.

❑ **Chain-referral schemes**—This fraud consists of buying an expensive article with the hope that the purchase of similar articles by friends will result in commissions to reduce the original price.

❑ **Vanity publishers**—This fraud involves the publication of a book or recording music which you have written. Victims are led to believe that their works have merit and are encouraged to invest money in the publication or recording.

❑ **Land fraud**—Retirement homesites are often the bait for "$1 Down and $10 a Month" ads. The low price is no reason to be less cautious about the purchase. You should ask yourself these questions:
   (a) What taxes will have to be paid?
   (b) What about the title to the land? Is it clear?
   (c) Have I been pressured into making a quick decision?

CONSUMER RESOURCES

The **Consumer Information Center**'s free handbook—Handbook, Pueblo, CO 81009—is a directory of Federal, state and local consumer offices, corporations' consumer offices, trade associations and dispute resolution programs. The revised version will highlight tips on how to use a credit card, complain about a defective product, select a financial institution and choose a school. Or on the net www.pueblo.gsa.gov

U.S. Consumer Gateway at www.consumer.gov provides a broad range of federal information, resources and tips to avoid scams.

   (d) Have I seen the land I want to buy?
   (e) Am I prepared to live in an isolated site, far from the city?
   (f) Is medical care available near the site?
   (g) Are utilities and facilities available?
   (h) How close will shopping facilities be?
   (i) Are improvements promised for the land in the near future?

❑ **Fake contest** where you have to pay for what you have "won."

❑ **Debt consolidation** where the consolidation fee is paid *before* money is applied to debts.

❑ **Charity rackets:**
   (a) Donate only to known causes and organizations.
   (b) Ask for a financial statement from unfamiliar organizations.
   (c) Check with the Better Business Bureau or Chamber of Commerce.

❑ **Fraudulent correspondence schools**—Watch the contract which must be signed, regardless of whether or not the individual wishes to continue with the course.

❑ **Memberships** in buyers, discount, recreational, or food distributors clubs, with representations that membership will result in savings.

The only protection you need is to be a little bit tougher, yourself.

Be hard to please. Insist on quality and service. Don't believe everything you hear or read. Complain.

Know how and where to file a complaint when your rights as a consumer have been violated. **It is worth the bother.**

Many times you can go back to the person who is responsible for the unsatisfactory service or the sale of a faulty product, and a courteous request on your part is all that is necessary.

HOW TO FILE A COMPLAINT

When you report unsatisfactory goods or services, assemble all the information about dates, payments, contracts, receipts, etc., so that there is little room for confusion. You will also impress the individual that you are serious about carrying through with your complaint by going to all that trouble!

If you cannot get satisfaction from the salesperson, find the highest authority to which you can appeal in the store. Keep calm. Maintaining your composure will show that you are confident.

Letters should be written to the President of the company. State the facts clearly. Keep a copy of everything for your records.

For complaints that cannot be settled using these measures, contact the Bureau of Consumer Fraud and Protection in your State Attorney General's office.

"I THINK YOU'LL FIND SIR, OUR BROCHURE SAYS SAFE BEACH...YOU MUST HAVE GONE INTO THE WATER!"

YOU'VE GOT YOUR HEALTH

"When you've got your health, you've got just about everything," we are told by television commercials. You may not be convinced that this is true, but would you agree that much of life is improved by having good health? What about your health? What are your chances of enjoying relatively good health during retirement?

George Gallup reported some time back that 60% of those over 60 were able to do physically almost anything they wanted to do. There is good indication that many people are enjoying full and satisfying lives, usually with some reminder from their body that they are driving a model whose parts don't function as they did when they were brand new.

By age 45, most people have one or more chronic conditions. Of those over 65, 81% report one or more chronic conditions. Only 49% reported any limitation on their activities by the chronic condition. Only 16% reported conditions which inhibited major activity on their part. A pattern is emerging as data is accumulated from the lives of those who achieve longevity.

PROFILE OF LONGEVITY

The individual most likely to succeed at living a long time has the following characteristics.

❑ Understanding of one's self: physically, mentally, and socially

❑ Good medical care in early and later life
❑ Heredity
❑ Environment
❑ Good health habits and personal care
❑ Healthy attitudes - a sense of humor
❑ Coping well with stress
❑ Daily exercise - walk every day
❑ Rewarding personal relationships
❑ A commitment to something other than ourselves
❑ Try something new
❑ Stimulate your brain - take a class, learn to play a musical instrument, learn a language

"YOU ARE WHAT YOU EAT"

Proper diet will have some effect on your body and your frame of mind. A proper diet is one of the principal contributors to good health. Unfortunately, it is more difficult to maintain during the years when your body needs all the help it can get…during retirement.

Food is expensive, and the reduced budget on which you live may tempt you to "cut corners" at mealtime. Besides, your appetite is not what it once was, and you may have developed a dislike for certain foods. It's just too much "bother" to prepare food for just the two of you (or just yourself).

Supermarkets are often inaccessible, and their packaged items are often too large for your needs, your kitchen equipment may not be adequate, etc. These may be reasons why you *don't* give your body the nutrients it requires to function well. Examine your diet to see that it provides both the energy and the nutrients you need. Check our suggestions under Consumer Education (Chapter 5) for ways of doing this without spending more for food.

The average American eats almost 1,500 pounds of food each year. We take in about 3,000 calories a day, when we could live longer if we reduced our intake by 23% to 2,300. This uniquely American problem of overeating gives the body more fuel than it can burn. It increases fat in the body, which interferes with the movement of muscles and places a burden on the heart. The increased demand for insulin, essential for burning fuel, causes a failure in the organs charged with its production.

TAKE IT OFF

If a major problem is eating too much, it can be corrected by *eating less*. Not necessarily! A diet is a prescription for a particular physical condition. It should be given the same respect as any other medical recommendation, both in the way it is received and the way it is followed. You don't prescribe medication or go to the inexperienced for medical advice. Don't give or take advice about dieting. "One man's meat is another man's poison" is a way of reminding us that we each require *individual* diagnosis and prescription.

About one older adult in three has a chronic health condition requiring diet as part of the treatment. The most common diets limit the intake of salt and fat. The large percentage of overweight Americans suggests a relationship between the number of diseases which are complicated by excess fat: the tendency toward heart attacks, cerebral hemorrhage, nephritis, and diabetes.

Diet counseling by a dietitian or nutritionist may be helpful in changing poor nutritional habits and adopting diets necessitated by disease. Insufficient exercise, diminished appetite, poor dentition, gastrointestinal problems, overweight, heart disease and diabetes—each make specific diet changes necessary. About 50% of Americans have lost all their teeth by age 85.

Good eating habits, including proper diet, will cut heart and vascular diseases by 25%. A decrease in respiratory diseases by 20% and arthritis and diabetes by 50% could be achieved by proper nutrition. Sometimes eating less, but more frequently, enables an individual to achieve the proper quantity of nutrients and energy with a minimum of anguish.

DON'T JUST SIT THERE!

Exercise is a vital necessity *every day*. You may be able to store the benefits of eating, but the benefits of exercise cannot be stored for long periods.

A physical fitness program has two goals: *organic fitness,* which includes the condition of the vital organs and limbs; and *dynamic fitness,* the efficiency of your heart and lungs.

You will be able to tell when your physical fitness program is having its desired effect. (People around you will also be able to tell!) Your attitude will be more positive and optimistic; you will accomplish more with less strain and tension.

When your body is functioning properly you will have greater stamina, strength, endurance

FOOD FOR LONGEVITY

The US Department of Agriculture recommends that your daily food consist of more greens, fruits and vegetables and fewer meats and dairy products. Select more food from the base of the pyramid and fewer as you go up.

- Cut down on Sodium.
- Drink eight glasses of water each day.
- If over 70 see your doctor about diet supplements.
- Read the Nutrition Facts on packaged foods.

Fats, Oils, Sweets
USE SPARINGLY

Milk, Yogurt & Cheese Group
2–3 SERVINGS

Vegetable Group
3–5 SERVINGS

Meat, Poultry, Fish, Dry Beans, Eggs & Nuts Group
2–3 SERVINGS

Fruit Group
2–4 SERVINGS

Bread, Cereal, Rice & Pasta Group
6–11 SERVINGS

and coordination. The times when you are "all thumbs" may be those in which you have not maintained a balanced program of exercise. And those joints!, how stiff they are after extended periods of inactivity: long trips, long sermons, etc.!! Regular exercise can bring back increased flexibility to most joints. For women, exercise decreases calcium loss from bones, thereby helping to prevent osteoporosis.

Chronic fatigue may be due to other causes, but much tiredness can be eliminated by greater activity! Read our suggestions as they relate to exercise.

An improved and more efficient circulatory system is another product of a good exercise program. Medical authorities suggest that the circulatory system of the average American male white-collar worker, aged 25, has the characteristics consistent with middle age.

The latest guidelines from federal health authorities and fitness experts stress that although strenuous exercise (such as jogging or cycling) provides the most benefits, more moderate exercise and even everyday physical activities (gardening, house cleaning, walking to work, or climbing a flight or two of stairs) can also help keep you healthy.

Exercise reduces the number of calories stored in your body as fat—keeping weight down and fitness up.

"AT EASE!"

Don't overdo exercise, particularly at the beginning. It took more than a day to get in your present condition, and it may take a while before you begin to look and feel better. Make your routine reasonable and (groan) fun. Join a group. Your local YMCA or high school may have an adult program. Persuade a friend to exercise with you. Get out and exercise with your dog, if you don't want to walk alone. Find an exercise show on TV, or do exercises watching the nightly news. Things may sound better with your circulation tuned up! Exercise is the conditioner for the healthy and therapy for the ill.

TURN BACK THE YEARS...

So you don't enjoy jogging miles every day—or you can't. You don't get a kick out of exhausting yourself on a tennis court. In fact, you don't do much of anything that involves physical exertion.

You have a problem, but fortunately it is one that can be solved easily and without cost, through regular exercise. As you grow older, exercise becomes more vital. Exercise is not a Fountain of Youth, but it can make later years easier and can prolong life.

A study of 300,000 men over 45 years old found that the death rate among those leading completely sedentary lives was four to five times that of men who exercise regularly. The study confirmed that bodies deteriorate— both men's and women's—without proper exercise. This is so whether you are in your 20's or up in your 70's or 80's. Bodies must be used. If they aren't, they lose efficiency and tone.

You can delay or reverse many of the deteriorating effects of age by exercising—alone, or even better with your spouse. All it takes is determination. It can be as easy and enjoyable as a half-hour walk four times a week.

AS YOU GROW OLDER

Dr. Herbert A. de Vries, director of the exercise laboratory of the Andrus Gerontology Center of the University of Southern California, recently outlined what happens to your body as you age, and how regular exercise can help in coping with changes:

❏ The heart's ability to pump blood declines by about 8% each decade in adulthood, and blood pressure increases as fatty deposits clog arteries. By middle-age, the openings of the coronary arteries are likely to be about 29% smaller than when you were in your mid 20's.

❏ Lung capacity decreases and the chest wall stiffens as you grow older; this cuts the amount of oxygen available to body tissues for work and other physical activities. The amount of oxygen you must use at age 75 is ordinarily less than half what it was at 20.

❑ Skeletal muscles, such as those in arms and legs, gradually lose strength. Tests show that 3% to 5% of muscle tissue is lost every decade. Loss of muscular strength and tissue mean ebbing endurance.

❑ The proportion of your body that is fat increases. To keep the same proportion of fat to lean body mass (not the way you look outside, but internally) you have to weigh less and less as you grow older.

Don't let these facts about aging worry you too much! Using your body can mitigate and delay the aging processes. You can continue to be youthful in spite of your calendar years.

ENHANCE YOUR VIGOR

Exercise can enhance the body's vigor and increase its work capacity. It can help the heart deliver more blood and oxygen for body tissues, slow the conversion of lean body mass to fat, and strengthen bones. It tends to stave off the aging of nerve cells, and, according to some medical opinion, it can slow down or avert arthritic changes in hips, knees, and other joints.

Swimming (a minimum quarter-mile), bicycling, folk and other dancing on a regular basis, and some less vigorous sports are good for everyone. So is gardening and—homemakers insist—work in the home.

Don't forget an exercise you do—or should do every day: *walking*. Walking has been long overlooked as an excellent exercise for the heart, muscles, and lungs, and can have added benefits as well. Walking can give you a chance to relax, enjoy your surroundings, and give you a much-needed "breath of fresh air." Build up your walking distance slowly, keeping your pace fast without becoming winded. Increase the distance you walk until you think you have exercised enough—45 minutes is a good limit for many people.

GET MOVING...BUT WISELY

We would all like to feel better and have our bodies be their best. What comes easiest for most of us is a regimen of regular exercise in the home to: tone muscles, prevent sagging posture, keep the heart strong and the joints flexible. Such a routine can be highly effective and, once you get into the swing of it, enjoyable and relaxing.

A word of caution: whatever you do, especially if you are over 40, should be undertaken with medical advice. This is critical if an exercise program or involvement in a sport is strenuous, and it is important even for an exercise program in the home. Your doctor may want to suggest special exercises for you, or caution you against undertaking too much.

YOUR HOME ROUTINE...

Exercise or physical fitness programs can be worked out for anyone—the middle-aged, the healthy aging and those with special health needs. Sit-down exercises for those in wheelchairs or who are otherwise sedentary are particularly important, as are exercises for the bedridden.

The Maryland Commission on Physical Fitness, with the help of the National Association for Human Development and the Maryland Office on Aging, has developed "The Basic Ten," a fitness program featured in an activity guide by the Michigan Office of Services to the Aging.

THE "BASIC TEN"

Before beginning the "Basic Ten":

❑ **See your doctor first.**

❑ Warm up before exercising. Breathe deeply, rising up on your toes slowly, with arms extended over your head, then exhale

THE BASIC TEN...

1 ARM SWINGS—Swing right arm rotating forward 5 times; reverse motion, rotating backward 5 times. Repeat with left arm. With both arms together in a windmill fashion swing forward 5 times.

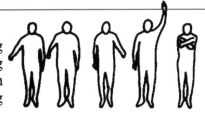

FINGER SQUEEZE—Extend arms shoulder height in front, palms down; squeeze the fingers slowly, then release. Repeat 5 times. Then turn palms up, squeeze fingers 5 times. Extend arms again in front and shake fingers 5 times. **2**

3 ARM TURNS—Extend arms to the side, palms up, cup hands, turn arms down in a circular movement and return to starting position. Repeat 5 times. Extend arms, cup hands, facing down, turn arms in the opposite direction 5 times.

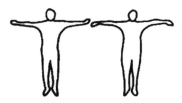

SHOULDER ROLLS—Beginning with arms at side, roll shoulders forward in full circle, slowly, 5 times; reverse by rolling shoulders backwards in a circle, slowly, 5 times. Then shrug shoulders up and down 5 times. **4**

5 BODY STRETCH—Extend right foot forward as far as it will go, leaving the left foot firmly planted; bend body forward with arms extended, stretch forward 5 counts, stretching further forward on each count. Reverse procedure. Lift up on your toes, stretch overhead to a count of 5.

...FOR PHYSICAL FITNESS

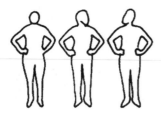

HEAD & NECK EXERCISE—Place hands on hips. Bend forward so that chin touches the chest. Then bend head to starting position and slowly turn the head to the left, return head to starting position and then slowly turn head to the right. Repeat 5 times.

6

7

EASY BACK STRETCH—Sit part way off the seat of a straight chair. Relax your body and let your head drop between your knees. Your shoulders should rest on your knees, your hands will hang alongside your legs. *Breathe naturally* while you relax in this position for two or three minutes. Then bring your hands up to your knees again, and *using your arms for support,* begin to curl yourself up to a sitting position, with your head straightening last.

BODY SIDE STRETCH—Place left hand on left hip, extend right arm over head, bend to left side toward the ground, to the count of two. Return to starting position and place right hand on right hip with left arm extended upward over head and bend to the right, to count of 2.

8

9

POSTURE EXERCISE—Stand erect with feet about six inches apart. Tighten leg muscles, tighten stomach by drawing it in, extend chest, bring arms up with clenched fists chest high, take deep breath, let it out slowly (keeping the muscles taut and rigid) vibrate arms back for a count of 3.

ARM STRETCH—With feet six inches apart, make fists, bend elbows, then thrust arms forward, bring back; thrust sideways, bring back, then thrust arms upward and down. Repeat 3 times.

10

slowly. Three times should do it. Also walk in place, lifting knees high ten times.

❑ Do your exercises slowly, and do not do too much for too long at first. *Stop* if you begin hurting anywhere or get tired. Increase your regimen gradually.

❑ Take deep breaths between exercises.

❑ You may feel some dizziness, which you can avoid by resting before alternating sides in an exercise.

❑ **15 to 20 minutes a day** will give you a good workout. Dr. de Vries suggests that you lie flat after each workout and take 15 minutes of yoga-like exercises: stretching leg muscles by bending legs from the hip and knee, tensing them as much as you can and holding them down with your arms.

Now, take a look at the "Basic Ten." Good luck, and happy exercising!

"AN APPLE A DAY, PLUS…"

Good nutrition is the cornerstone of a happy, healthy life and is instrumental in disease prevention and control. Preventative health measures include more than the regular consumption of apples. There are precautions we can take to reduce the probability that we will lose our health through sickness or accidents. We can increase our resistance to illness and make early detection and treatment work against many disabilities.

EARLY TO BED

It isn't so important what time you get there, as it is how long you stay there. Older people generally need *less* sleep than middle-aged and younger people. Individual requirements differ, but 7-8 hours during a 24-hour period is about average. Scientists have observed that cumulative sleep loss can lead to nervousness and psychosomatic illness. Chronic inability to sleep suggests the need for a doctor's attention. *Too much sleep* can be a problem, indicating boredom or illness.

FOR A GOOD NIGHT'S SLEEP

If you are more than occasionally experiencing trouble falling asleep and sleeping well, if it is a frequently recurring, long-lasting chronic problem that you can't shake, see your doctor. It is better to be assured that you haven't anything to worry about than to find out later that you have a problem that requires professional treatment.

HAZARDS TO GOOD SLEEP

Drs. Joyce and Anthony Kales, who conduct sleep research at the Hershey Medical Center of Pennsylvania State University, have found that many chronic insomniacs keep their problems

"bottled up inside," without venting anger, frustrations and disappointments.

According to the Kales, tension, stress and anxiety build-up are carried into the night. They are likely to cause racing thoughts, activate the physical arousal system and make it difficult to get to sleep. Body temperature and heart rates go up for disturbed chronic insomniacs, and can lead to neurotic depression and emotional problems.

Chronic insomnia often can be traced to illnesses such as angina, asthma, other respiratory disorders, or to back problems or arthritis. If you suffer persistent sleeplessness see your doctor. Prescribed medication often helps.

There are clinics around the country where technicians can diagnose sleep problems and help resolve them. Here are some suggestions outlined by Dr. Donald Douglas of the Lenox Hill Hospital in New York, Drs. Joyce and Anthony Kales of the Pennsylvania Hershey Medical Center, Wallace Mendelson of the National Institute of Mental Health and others in the field:

- ❑ Recognize that sleep needs differ; you may be among those who need less than a seven and one-half hour norm.
- ❑ Go to bed and get up about the same time every day, weekends included.
- ❑ If you go to bed and don't feel sleepy, try to lull yourself to sleep with a book that isn't so absorbing that it keeps you awake instead of making you sleepy. Or turn on quiet, soothing music.
- ❑ Drink warm milk. It has an essential amino acid that has been used medically to treat depression and as a sedative. Although milk

has only a small amount of amino acid (medically referred to as L-tryptophan) it often helps assure restful sleep. Some drinks, like a "hot toddy," may help you fall asleep, but the sleep you get will be less restful. It is best to avoid alcohol before heading to bed.

- ❑ Relax in bed and try to be absolutely still. Because the body naturally resists non-movement, each time one moves in trying to find a sleep-inducing position one must start over again to relax the body and the mind.
- ❑ Concentrate on breathing, inhaling and exhaling deeper, and at regular intervals; think of your breathing, trying to keep your mind clear of disturbing thoughts; your grandmother probably called this "counting sheep."
- ❑ Don't try to force sleep. The more you struggle to sleep, or worry about wakefulness, the harder it will be to get to sleep. It can be better to relax and stay awake a while longer.
- ❑ Don't resort to pills *unless* they've been prescribed by your doctor. Though over-the-counter remedies to promote quick sleep and restful nights can be useful for occasional sleeplessness, the National Institute of Health has warned that sleeping pills, or even mild remedies, can be harmful if overused. If you can tolerate aspirin, you might try it as a relaxant at bedtime, when you need one.

For more information and brochures on sleep difficulties, write to: The National Sleep Foundation, 1522 K Street, NW, Suite 500, Washington, DC 20005. Or on the internet: www.sleepfoundation.org.

ZZZZZZZZZZZZ·**DO'S AND DONT'S ABOUT SLEEP!**

NO ONE CAN SAVE YOUR EYES BUT YOU

ARE YOU AT A HIGH RISK FOR GLAUCOMA ?

OVER 35?

OVER 65?

HIGH BLOOD PRESSURE?

FAMILY HISTORY OF GLAUCOMA?

SURGERY OR EYE INJURY?

TAKING CORTISONE?

CHECK FOR GLAUCOMA EVERY 2 YEARS

CHECK ONE: HIGH RISK

CHECK TWO: VERY HIGH RISK

STOP SMOKING

Smokers are becoming a minority—only one-third of adults are now cigarette smokers. If you still smoke, now's the time to join the more than 30 million ex-smokers. Smoking is an expensive habit, both in terms of your health and your wealth. It's responsible for more cancer-related deaths than any other single agent, and it's a contributing factor in emphysema, bronchitis, and heart attack.

You know you should quit. Let's accentuate the positive. Think of the benefits of quitting now.

When you quit smoking, your body starts to repair itself almost immediately. You enter lower risk groups. You lose your smoker's hacking cough, and related head and stomach aches. You recover your sense of taste and smell. And at over $3 a pack, smoking is one habit you can afford to lose.

The American Cancer Society has information to help you. Contact your local chapter.

MENTAL AND PHYSICAL HEALTH

Mental and physical condition are too complicated to discuss at length in this chapter. Most of us have sensed the effect which illness in one area has upon well-being in the other. The person with a healthy self-concept and social adjustment will not be completely protected from poor health. But those who cope successfully with life's

problems, not only during aging, but throughout all of life, usually are more positive about themselves. Just as you have probably faced crises or problematic situations during your life, you will face them in retirement and cope with them as effectively as you did earlier.

PROFILE OF A HEALTHY LIFE

People with the following traits tend to adjust and cope better than those who lack them. Check those that describe you:

❑ Enduring and honest affection for others
❑ Independent
❑ Has satisfying outlets for time and energy
❑ Enjoys life
❑ Has a sense of usefulness
❑ Avoids self-pity.

INVISIBLE SUPPORTS

The person who discovers meaning in life has the resources which are not available to the skeptic. Some individuals develop these through their life experiences, while others are sustained by confidence in God.

Dr. Carl Jung, one of psychiatry's founders, said, "Among all my patients, in the second half of life … that is to say, over thirty-five, there has not been one whose problem in the last resort was not that of finding a religious outlook on life. It is safe to say that every one of them feel ill because he had lost that which the living religions of every age have given their followers, and none of them has really been healed who did not regain his religious outlook."

LIVING WITH STRESS

Stress is the body's physical and chemical reaction to anything that frightens, excites, confuses or endangers a person.

No matter what you do on the job or away from it, you may come under mental or physical stress. Although stress is not necessarily a medical problem, it can be. It must be watched.

Tolerable stress promotes physical and mental development and growth. The adrenaline pumped into the bloodstream at such times can give the extra strength needed to achieve more—to endure more, work harder and more creatively.

Stress can be a prod, but if it gets out of hand it can be harmful.

Studies conducted by the Harvard University Medical School, Boston University and Northwestern University found strong evidence that prolonged and excessive stress can be a serious health concern—even a killer. It can make men and women more susceptible to a wide variety of diseases, including cancer.

THE "BLAHS"...OR WORSE

In its milder forms, stress usually leads to nothing worse than a persistent case of the "blahs," or general unhappiness, depression and nagging anxieties. The serious problems come when *stress* is allowed to become *distress*—when the body and mind no longer can handle it. Once it passes the level of tolerance, it becomes a potential medical problem.

Stress can cause changes in the body's immune system and reduce the body's ability to fight virus-infected cells. According to Harvard's Dr. Steve

Locke, this can "pre-dispose a person to illness."

Stress affects the old and the young, but because the young usually have more physical resilience they are better able to cope with it. Those approaching retirement, men and women, or retirees are the most vulnerable.

As we grow older, says Dr. Ruth B. Weg of the University of California's Andrus Gerontology Center, we have "a diminishing ability to respond to stress." It hits harder and recovery takes longer.

We must watch ourselves more closely as we grow older, learn to recognize the symptoms of stress. Learn to cope with stress before it builds up dangerously.

RECOGNIZING THE SYMPTOMS

Unfortunately, too many of us do not recognize the signs of stress, or pay too little attention to them. For far too many, it's a natural part of the wear and tear of life—something that must be endured.

Recognizing the signs of stress is the first step toward coping with it effectively.

What are the symptoms? "Butterflies" in the stomach. Tension and nervousness over prolonged periods. Light perspiration when things don't seem to be going right. Headaches. A feeling of pressure on the back of the neck. Heavy breathing. Or an "internal racing" and pounding heart.

We may be alerted to stress by insomnia, ulcers and other stomach troubles. We may find it's the cause of hypertension and heart strain, or a change to an unhealthy pattern of behavior, such as excessive smoking, drinking or eating in search of relief. A sudden urge for snacking could signal stress!

Recognize that stress is a problem that must be dealt with, to minimize the way it affects you.

HOW TO EASE STRESS

Start by seeking the cause of stress. Often it's obvious. Sometimes it isn't.

The death or serious illness of a spouse is considered by psychologists to be the most serious cause of stress. On a scale of 100, other causes are rated substantially lower.

The loss of a spouse, or the death of a close relative or friend, is the hardest to handle. Help should be sought.

Other major causes of stress include retirement—rated high on the stress scale because of the upheaval it causes in personal lives—illness and accidents, marital troubles and divorce, sexual difficulties, financial problems, job worries, work-related problems and changes in living conditions.

Unlike the death of a spouse, these are seldom serious enough, alone, to cause major problems. When one stressful situation comes, others often follow. The loss of a job, 47 on the stress scale, can cause financial problems, disrupt living patterns and lead to all sorts of satellite problems, sending the stress count above 200—a critical level.

Studies that have concentrated on the causes of serious stress have found that 27% of a group interviewed intensively had experienced "high levels of psychic distress" over a year's time as a result of a steady buildup of stress.

Stress takes two basic forms: Mental stress and physical stress.

❏ Mental stress is a "bad" stress, caused primarily by emotional disturbances, frustrations or anxieties—things over which we have little or no control. These feelings of stress can be serious and need prompt attention.

❏ Physical stress is a "good" stress, as long as you don't overexert yourself. While it can be serious in later years, it can also be relaxing and an antidote for mental stress.

Rest is good in cases of physical stress—but physical activity, even to a point of careful stress, is helpful when mental stress is a problem. Don't sit and worry; do something involving physical activity.

STRESS: WORK IT OFF

In retirement, recognize that boredom from inactivity is stressful; work it off. Everyday activities such as gardening, chores around the home, walking or a physical hobby will suffice.

Exertion is not always necessary. The concentration needed for chess or some other game, a crossword puzzle or reading can help.

Often, simply blowing off steam can help relieve stress. Repressed anger, frustration and anxiety make it build up in daily life. Some therapists advocate going into a room, closing doors and windows, and letting off a "primal scream" to ease pressures. That sounds extreme. Find your own way, but get rid of stress—and develop ways to avoid its return.

Stress, that leads to muscular contractions and aches and tension headaches, can be eased by medication, usually aspirin if you can take it, but don't be a pill-popper. Medication may ease stress

WHAT YOU CAN DO WHEN YOU FEEL *STRESS* COMING ON!

TALK IT OUT! — LET'S DO THIS! / GOOD IDEA!

RELAX! — HONK! / SCREECH! / BEEP!

PLAN! — TULIPS! / ...AND ROSES! / SPRING PLANTING

ENJOY! — THIS IS A DELICIOUS RECIPE! / THANK YOU!

BILL KRESSE

TEST YOUR STRESS LEVEL

Score Yourself: Never = 0; Seldom = 1; Frequently = 2

How often do you feel:

Strong anxiety ....( )
Irritable over little things ....( )
Frustrated ....( )
Quick anger ....( )
A desire to avoid people ....( )
A difficulty in concentrating.....................( )
Easily disturbed or startled ....( )
Jittery, unable to sit still..........................( )
Unusually emotional ....( )
Depressed ....( )
A loss of interest in everything................( )
Persistently keyed up ....( )

How often do you experience:

General fatigue...( )
Sleeplessness at night ....( )
Heart pounding ....( )
Headaches ....( )
Breathing difficulties ....( )
Burping, gassiness, acid stomach ....( )
Frequent need to urinate ....( )
Tense head and neck muscles ....( )
Grinding of teeth......................................( )
Dry mouth or throat ....( )
Sudden perspiration ....( )
Cold hands or feet if it's warm,
 sweaty hands or feet otherwise ....( )

Add the point totals in the two columns: If together they are 10 or under, you are normal;
if 10 to 20, take care; if higher, you could have a problem.

symptoms but it does not attack the cause of the stress, and it can be habit-forming and lead to a different form of personal stress.

Consider aspirin or anti-depressant or anti-anxiety drugs (they should be prescribed by a doctor) as only temporary relief for stress. Seek real relief, not from pills, but from the causes of the stress you feel.

Rest is important to relieve physical stress. It can also be important in situations involving mental and emotional stress: Lack of sleep or rest aggravates tensions and the body's ability to throw them off. However, sleep does not necessarily attack the causes of stress; the tension headaches or tight muscles you have at bedtime often return after you awaken.

Stress also leads to night wakefulness. If you can't get the seven or eight hours of sleep you need, consult your doctor.

If you can isolate what is bothering you, the cause of your stress, try to work out a solution. If there are a number of causes, work on them one at a time, the most important first. Learn to accept what you cannot change, problems beyond your control, until you are better able to do something about them.

If you can't seem to work things out on your own, talk to a sympathetic listener, someone you respect and trust. It will help put things in better perspective. The listener can be a member of your family, a friend, a clergyman or teacher, someone in the personnel office, or your doctor.

SERIOUS STRESS: TALK IT OUT

If professional counseling seems wise, there are Family Service and other similar agencies available.

Don't feel ashamed, embarrassed or guilty about going to a professional for assistance; it's not an admission of personal inadequacy but a mark of intelligence to seek advice. Dr. Locke of Harvard says, "to the extent that an individual has effective coping strategies and social psychological resources to rely on, stress should cause less deterioration of health and well-being."

WHEN STRESS BUILDS UP

Try to relax. Slow down: Don't rush your life away. As a cardiologist put it, don't let yourself become a heart-attack-prone person—one who is hurried, aggressive, impatient and easily angered. A more relaxed person lives a far more pleasant and healthier life.

A relaxing technique is the "rag doll" exercise. Sit on the edge of a straight chair, knees about 12 inches apart, legs slanted out 10 or 12 inches in front of the chair. Sit straight and then collapse forward, back rounded, hands resting on your knees. Let your mind concentrate on parts of your body, relaxing each in turn, breathing deeply. Do this whenever you feel a need to ease body tensions. It will work.

Rid yourself of trivial obligations. Concentrate on what is most important to you.

Cultivate diversions, such as concerts, plays, visits to museums, visits with friends—and sports as a spectator rather than as a fiercely competitive participant.

Learn to enjoy your own company; do nothing rather than rush to keep up with a full calendar.

Learn a few secrets that can help fight stress. One is a quick-quieting, ten second breathing exercise: When you feel stress coming on, take two slow, easy, deep breaths and exhale slowly, a count of four in, four out, four in and four out again. As you exhale, let your body go limp. Let your mind relax, also. You can feel better immediately once you learn to relax completely.

In prolonged periods of stress, this can be done frequently during the day—but it shouldn't become a scheduled exercise, every half-hour or hour, say, but enjoyed as a "break" in times of pressure.

COPING WITH DEPRESSION

"You've got a bad case of the blues."
"I'm down deep in the dumps."

You hear people say such things. Chances are you say them yourself, at times. It happens to everyone.

If it is a mood that comes and goes, you can fight it off by thinking and acting positively. If it doesn't go away, you should be aware that depression can be a major mental health problem.

It affects more than your mood. It can manifest itself in symptoms as diverse as sleeplessness (you lie awake worrying about real or fancied problems), boredom, inertia and an inability to concentrate, impatience and irritability and not uncommonly, stress. It can affect your appetite; you might lose interest in food.

It can lead to more smoking or drinking. It can be a factor in driving. Accident records indicate that drivers suffering from depression are more likely to be reckless and to lack the concentration vital for safety. It can affect performance on the job.

THE BLUES OR DEPRESSION

New York University's Medical Center has been conducting intensive research into depression through its Millhauser Laboratories. This research has resulted in more accurate diagnoses and more effective treatments.

Irene Chang, coordinator of the depression studies program has circulated a checklist of possible symptoms that warrant the attention of those 55 or older—and younger persons who might benefit from early recognition of depression problems.

The symptoms of depression include:

❑ A low mood—feeling sad, blue and/or hopeless much of the time.

❑ Appetite disturbance—a poor appetite or an increased appetite.

❑ Sleep problems—difficulty falling asleep, waking up during the night or waking early.

❑ Lack of energy—quickly fatigued, tired for no reason, tense, with difficulty relaxing.

❑ Loss of interest in usual activities.

❑ Feelings of self-reproach or inappropriate guilt.

❑ Trouble concentrating and possible difficulties making decisions.

❑ Excessive thoughts of death or that life is not worth living.

If you checked off four or more see a physician.

THE BLUES...GET RID OF THEM

The symptoms for the plain old blues or blahs are much the same as those for more serious forms of depression. The big difference is how frequently they recur and in how many ways.

Millions of Americans suffer now and then from the blues. Worrying minds make us sleepless, sap our strength, cause us to lose interest in food and usual interests and otherwise have an impact similar to depression. However, in most instances you can fight off the blues. It's not always easy. You have to concentrate on positive thinking instead of worrying about troubles you can do nothing about.

NYU's Depression Studies Program suggests:

❑ Don't knock yourself.

❑ Don't build up a problem by going over it time and again; you're likely to make it worse, not better.

❑ Share your feelings with others; your spouse, a relative, a friend or a consultant is likely to have good advice.

❑ Don't use your age as an excuse for being "down," mentally or physically.

❑ Give yourself credit for what you've accomplished through the years—and what you can continue to contribute.

❑ If your blues are about imminent retirement, get rid of them; approach retirement positively as something you can make comfortable and happy.

CHECKLIST FOR HEALTH

Do you: Limit salt, sugar, fat, red meat?
Yes ☐   No ☐

Eat a balanced diet: milk, milk products, meat, poultry, fish, fruits, vegetables and grains?
Yes ☐   No ☐

Make mealtime a pleasure?
Yes ☐   No ☐

Limit coffee and alcohol to two drinks per day?
Yes ☐   No ☐

Control medication?
Yes ☐   No ☐

Not smoke?
Yes ☐   No ☐

Control weight and exercise regularly?
Yes ☐   No ☐

Have stress under control?
Yes ☐   No ☐

Relax easily and laugh frequently?
Yes ☐   No ☐

Have a stable emotional life?
Yes ☐   No ☐

Sleep well?
Yes ☐   No ☐

Participate in community activities?
Yes ☐   No ☐

Have regular check-ups?
Yes ☐   No ☐

Keep mentally active: reading, studying, attending discussions and cultural events?
Yes ☐   No ☐

CHAPTER 7: HEALTH INSURANCE

MEDICARE

Medicare is a government sponsored health insurance program available to Americans, 65 and older, to severely disabled persons under 65 and those with End-Stage Renal Disease. Medicare has two parts: hospital insurance (Medicare Part A) and medical insurance (Medicare Part B).

Medicare's hospital insurance component (Part A) covers a significant portion of hospitalization costs and also helps pay for certain follow-up care after you leave the hospital.

MEDICARE PART B INSURANCE

Traditional Medicare Part B medical insurance is a "fee-for-service" program. You visit the doctor of your choice. Medicare pays for 80% of the approved amount for the cost of the service; you pay the remaining 20% (there is a $100 annual deductible). Your doctor may charge higher than the approved amount (check in advance); in this case, you, not Medicare, must pay more. Under traditional Medicare, doctors are restricted in how much they can charge Medicare patients (but they are not required to see Medicare patients).

Medicare Part B helps pay for laboratory tests, x-rays and some medical equipment which is necessary. Prescription medications are not covered under Medicare Part B, and screening tests, such as cholesterol testing, are not automatically covered.

If you request screening tests, or your doctor recommends them, you may be responsible for payment. Reimbursement for some screening tests, for example, mammograms, pelvic examinations, screening for colon and rectal cancer and measurement of bone density for women are now available.

ENROLLMENT INFORMATION

Hospital insurance (Medicare Part A) is available to anyone who is eligible for Social Security benefits. You do not have to retire to get hospital insurance. It is available **free** at age 65, **but you must enroll.** Check with your Social Security office **three months before** you reach age 65. People who have not worked long enough to qualify for Social Security can buy Medicare Part A insurance by paying a monthly premium.

Medical insurance (Medicare Part B) is available to anyone who is 65 or older. You pay a monthly premium. If you were covered for medical insurance by your employer while working and will still be covered in retirement, signing up for Medicare Part B insurance may not be necessary. You'll save the monthly premium.

Medical insurance has a 7 month initial enrollment period. This period begins **three months before** you turn 65. For example, if you turn 65 on April 11th, the enrollment period begins January 1st, and lasts until July 31st. If you turn down medical insurance and then decide you want it after your 7 month initial enrollment period ends, you can sign up during a general enrollment period—January 1 through March 31 of each year. However, if you enroll during a general enrollment period, your medical insurance protection **won't start until the following July, and your premium will be 10 percent higher** for each 12 month period you could have been enrolled, but were not.

Those who have opted for early retirement benefits under Social Security or Railroad Retirement are automatically enrolled in Medicare Part B when they reach age 65. Monthly premiums are deducted from Social Security checks. Medicare Hotline: 800-638-6833.

MEDICARE (PART A) HOSPITAL INSURANCE: COVERED SERVICES PER BENEFIT PERIOD [1]

Service	Benefits	Medicare Pays**	You Pay**
HOSPITALIZATION Semi-private room and board, general nursing, and miscellaneous hospital services and supplies	First 60 days 61st day to 90th day 91st day to 150th day* Beyond 150 days	All but $776 All but $194 per day All but $388 per day Nothing	$776 $194 per day $388 per day All costs
POST HOSPITAL SKILLED NURSING FACILITY CARE In a facility approved by Medicare. You must have been in a hospital for at least 3 days and enter the facility within 30 days after hospital discharge (2) and with the same diagnosis as leaving the hospital	First 20 days	100% of approved amount	Nothing
	Additional 80 days	All but $97.00 per day	$97.00 per day
	Beyond 100 days	Nothing	All costs
HOME HEALTH CARE Medicare pays intermittent visits for skilled nursing care or physical therapy	Unlimited visits as medically necessary	Full Cost	Nothing
HOSPICE CARE	Two 90-day periods and one 30-day period	All but limited costs for outpatient drugs and inpatient respite care	Limited cost sharing for outpatient drugs and inpatient respite care
BLOOD	Blood	All but first 3 pints	For first 3 pints

People not eligible for Social Security benefits can purchase Medicare Part A Hospital Insurance for $301 per month (for those with less than 30 credits) or $166 per month (for those with 30-39 credits).

* 60 Reserve Days may be used only once: days used are not renewable.

** These figures are subject to change each year.

(1) A Benefit Period begins on the first day you receive service as an inpatient in a hospital and ends after you have been out of the hospital or skilled nursing facility for 60 days in a row.

(2) Medicare and private insurance will not pay for most nursing home care. You pay for custodial care and most care in a nursing home. There are now some policies on the market which will pay for all nursing home costs but they are very expensive.

(3) Medicare pays processing costs; if you have donors to replace the blood, it would cost you nothing.

MEDICARE (PART B) MEDICAL INSURANCE: COVERED SERVICES PER BENEFIT YEAR *

Service	Benefits	Medicare Pays	You Pay
MEDICAL EXPENSE Physician's services, inpatient and outpatient medical services and supplies, physical and speech therapy, ambulance, chiropractic (limited), occupational therapy, durable medical equipment, prosthetic devices, second opinion before surgery, podiatrist's services, diagnostic laboratory tests, etc.	Medicare pays for medical services in or out of the hospital. Some insurance policies pay less (or nothing) for hospital outpatient medical services or services in a doctor's office	80% of approved amount (after $100 deductible)	$100 deductible ** plus 20% of balance of approved amount (Plus any charge above approved amount) ***
HOME HEALTH CARE Intermittent visits for skilled nursing care or physical therapy	Unlimited visits as medically necessary	Full Cost	Nothing
OUTPATIENT HOSPITAL TREATMENT	Unlimited as medically necessary	80% of approved amount (after $100 deductible)	Subject to deductible plus 20% of balance of approved amount
BLOOD	Blood	80% of approved amount (after first 3 pints)	For first 3 pints ††† plus 20% of balance of approved amount

* Available at a monthly premium in 2000 for $45.50.

** Once you have paid $100 for covered services, the Part B deductible does not apply to further covered services the rest of the year.

*** You pay for charges greater than the amount approved by Medicare, unless the doctor or supplier agrees to accept Medicare's approved amount as the total charge for services rendered. Always ask you doctor or supplier to accept assignment. Assignment means the doctor or supplier accepts as full payment whatever the Medicare allowed charge is, and can bill you only the $100 deductible, if not already paid, plus the 20% co-insurance.

††† There is only one deductible for blood each year. If you meet the blood deductible under Part A, you do not have to meet it again under Part B.

NEW MEDICARE BENEFITS

Annual mammograms to screen for breast cancer for women 40 and older. There is a 20% copay.

Annual Pap smears and pelvic examinations to detect vaginal and cervical cancer for **high risk women**.

Pap smears and pelvic examinations to detect vaginal and cervical cancer for **low risk women every three years**.

Screening for colon and rectal cancer.

Diabetes self management supplies, such as glucose monitors, lancets, and test strips and self management training for patients are fully covered. A person does not need to be using insulin to get these benefits.

Bone mass measurements for those at high risk of developing osteoporosis.

Annual prostate screening for men over 50

Flu, Pneumonia & Hepatitis B Shots

NOT COVERED BY MEDICARE

- ❏ Private duty nursing
- ❏ Hospital telephone and television
- ❏ Private hospital room
- ❏ Most prescription drugs
- ❏ Custodial care in a nursing home
- ❏ Custodial care at home
- ❏ Most preventive care
- ❏ Most chiropractic services
- ❏ Cosmetic surgery
- ❏ Care outside of the United States
- ❏ Acupuncture
- ❏ Hearing aids
- ❏ Eyeglasses
- ❏ Experimental procedures
- ❏ Dental Care

MEDIGAP INSURANCE POLICIES

It is important to note that Medicare Part A and traditional Medicare Part B benefits **do not cover all health care costs.** In many cases, these additional costs can be quite substantial, which is why many insurance companies now offer "Medigap" policies covering cost not covered by Medicare.

Medigap policies range in cost from $400 to $1,800 per year. All policies cover a basic core of services currently not paid in full by Medicare. More expensive policies may pay for doctor's charges above Medicare's proscribed amounts, and other benefits you may or may not require.

If you decide you need a Medigap policy, **shop around**, and buy a policy that offers you only what you need.

Medigap Premiums, although the benefits are identical for all Medigap plans of the same type, the premiums may vary greatly from one company to another and from area to area. Insurance companies use three different methods to calculate premiums: issue age, attained age and no age rating.

If your company uses the issues age method and you were 65 when you bought the policy, you will always pay the same premium the company charges people who are 65 regardless of your age. If it uses the attained age method, the premium is based on your current age and will increase as your grow older. Under the no age rating, everyone pays the same premium regardless of age. Your state insurance department must approve the rates charged for all Medigap policies. The insurance company can raise your premiums only when it has approval to raise the premiums for everyone else with the same policy.

If you opt for an alternative to traditional Part B Medicare medical insurance, you may not need any Medigap policy at all.

IMPORTANT: You cannot be turned down for Medigap insurance if you apply *within* six

months after you reach age 65. After that, insurers, with certain important exceptions, may turn you down (see HMO Concerns page 69).

MEDICAID

Medicaid is a program of assistance to those of any age who need medical services they cannot afford.

There are income and net worth limits for Medicaid eligibility, which differ from state to state. Essentially, a Medicaid recipient and spouse may have income up to a certain amount and also retain assets up to a certain amount, including one's home, and be eligible for Medicaid. Medicaid rules are very complicated. Check with your attorney, senior center, or your local government Office of Aging for specific details. **Check now** so you're prepared when and if you may need Medicaid in the future.

As Medicare does not cover long-term nursing home custodial care, which can be quite costly, Medicaid is often the only option for those who find they need such care.

It is important to keep in mind that you are not expected to exhaust your life savings, go into debt, or sell your home before receiving Medicaid. A lien may be placed on your home to reimburse the state for your expenses.

LONG TERM CARE INSURANCE

Neither Medicare, Medigap nor HMO's will cover non-medical at home care or the full costs of nursing home expenses. There are long term care policies that help protect your assets that might have to be liquidated in order to pay the high costs of nursing home care. The policies which vary in coverage are less expensive when purchased at an earlier age. Be sure to purchase one that does not raise the premiums as you grow older. Be careful, the policies are very complicated. Don't be pressured into buying one. For you it might not be a good deal.

MEDICARE HMO

Currently, 17% of Medicare enrollees opt to join a Medicare Health Maintenance Organization (HMO) instead of the traditional "fee-for-service" program. It is important to note that there is no standard HMO. Plans vary widely in terms of services offered, the quality of those services, and amounts charged.

Some HMOs offer more benefits than does traditional Medicare and do so at a lower cost to the patient, others are reducing their benefits; while still others are withdrawing coverage completely in certain geographical areas.

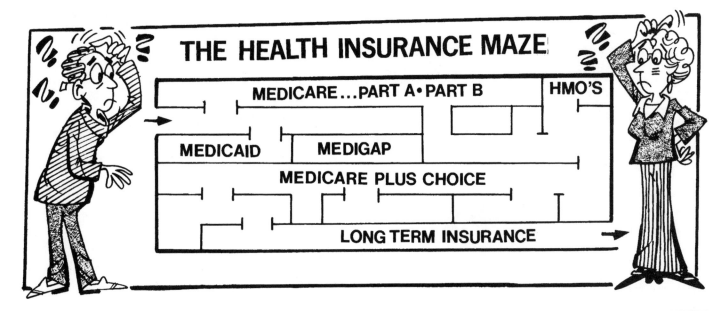

WHERE TO FIND GUIDANCE

Medicare Compare (free)
Medicare Hotline (800) 633-4227

**Managed Care: A Guide for Medicare
Beneficiaries** (free)
AARP, Publication No. D15595
601 E St., NW
Washington, DC 20049

**Medicare HMOs: Your Rights, Risks
&Obligations** ($6)
Medicare Rights Center, Box A,
1460 Broadway, 11th Fl.,
New York, NY 10036
www.medicarerights.org

**The National Committee for Quality
Assurance** (NCQA) (free)
list of HMOs and their accreditation status
(888) 275-7585 or www.ncqa.org

The National Research Corporation
(402) 475 2525 or www.nationalresearch.com

Medicare Hotline:
(800) 638-6833 or www.medicare.gov.

**Your State Health Department or
State Insurance Department**

In an HMO, health care providers are banded into a network. You are assigned a **primary care physician** (some plans may use a nurse practitioner working with a physician) who coordinates your health care through this network. The primary care physician takes care of your routine medical needs. To see a specialist, you must first gain the permission of the primary care physician (who in turn may need to gain approval from an HMO administrator).

If you select an HMO, your Medicare Part B premium remains the same. Medicare pays the HMO, on your behalf, a monthly premium that covers both Part A and Part B coverage. It is important to note that Medicare HMOs offer all traditional Medicare benefits (Part A hospital insurance plus Part B medical insurance), usually without deductibles or co-payments. Thus, the need for a Medigap policy is eliminated. But, **don't drop your Medigap policy**, you might want to keep it for awhile. You currently can switch from an HMO to fee-for-service Medicare, but since you might face problems getting a Medigap policy if your health has changed. It may be a good idea to continue your Medigap policy for a few months while you experience the services from your HMO.
Medicare HMOs usually offer additional benefits not generally covered by Medicare (preventive care, eye care, prescription drugs, inoculations, etc.). Enrollment in an HMO may provide access to a broader array of health services at an overall lower cost. Some HMOs may charge you a monthly amount beyond the premium Medicare pays the plan for these added services. Check for these changes in benefits and costs.

HOW HMOs WORK

It is important to understand how an individual HMO is paid by Medicare, and, in turn, how it pays its participating physicians.

Some plans put the doctor "at risk". They pay the doctor a set amount for each Medicare patient assigned. If the cost of the service is less, the doctor wins; if the costs of the service is higher, the doctor loses. These plans are called capitated plans, because doctors are paid on a per person or per capita basis. Doctors have a financial interest in limiting your access to expensive care. You should exercise caution with plans that pay their participating physicians bonuses for limiting expensive care.

"Non-capitated" plans pay the provider only when the beneficiary uses services, and a larger co-payment may be required. Generally, better plans pay their health care providers according to the services they provide. If you visit the doctor, he gets paid; if you don't visit, he doesn't get paid. This is good because it will motivate the doctor to want to see you (you usually will have to pay a modest co-payment). Some other "non-capitated" plans simply pay their doctors a salary, which relieves negative financial pressures on their decisions concerning your medical care.

In assessing an HMO, focus on its reputation for promptly providing needed services regardless of the cost involved. An HMOs service ethic is ultimately the most decisive factor in judging its appropriateness for you. **Health care is more than a financial decision.**

HMO CONCERNS

There are hundreds of HMOs nationwide (and soon, with the advent of PPOs and PSOs, there will be many more see page 70). Some are better than others. The central issues in determining

> ## IT'S A GOOD IDEA...
> to bring your medicines with you to your doctor's appointment for review.

whether an HMO is good are: Are the plan's doctors qualified? Are its affiliated hospitals well-recommended? Will you be able to see your primary care physician without delay? Will you get access to specialist care in a timely manner when you need it?

This last question is particularly crucial, as medicine operates in a "gray area." It is not always clear that specialist care is needed. The use of specialized care has driven up the cost of health care for all of us. But has a particular HMO gone too far? Does it deny access to reasonable care? The only way to determine this is to ask around. What has been the experience of your friends and neighbors? Talk to doctors inside and outside the plan. Find out what percentage of the HMO's members have dropped their coverage in the past year. If this number is greater than 15%, watch out. In short, before joining an HMO, do your homework.

If you do join an HMO, and you are not satisfied, you are free to switch to a different HMO or sign-up for traditional Medicare fee-for-service insurance. You will have to provide your HMO notice and, probably more so in future

LIST YOUR PROBLEMS *BEFORE* THE DOCTORS VISIT!

DON'T FORGET... ...YOU LOST WEIGHT!

BAD BACK I CAN'T SLEEP!

BESIDES MY BACK, I HAVEN'T SLEPT WELL!

DR. T......

BAD BACK CAN'T SLEEP

B.K.

MEDICARE + CHOICE

HMO: A Health Maintenance Organization is organized by an insurance company, which bands doctors and hospitals into a network. The employer, individual or Medicare pays the HMO and the HMO takes responsibility for much of the members' health care costs. HMOs limit the expense of care by disciplining doctors in their network and limiting members' access to care outside the network. HMOs provide preventive care and cover a wider range of costs than traditional fee-for-service Medicare insurance. Many are reducing their benefits.

Point-of-Service (POS) Plan: This option is now offered by many HMOs. HMO members who select a POS option pay a higher monthly premium but have greater flexibility in seeing doctors outside the HMO's network.

Preferred Provider Organization (PPO): An HMO-type organization established by an insurance company but more loosely organized, allowing members greater flexibility in seeing doctors outside the HMO's network.

Provider Sponsored Organization (PSO): PSOs are another type of HMO except they are run by medical providers themselves—doctors and hospitals.

Staff/Group Model HMO: An HMO with salaried health care providers.

Medical Savings Account (MSA) You choose a medicare approved insurance policy with a very high annual deductible. Medicare pays the premiums for this policy. The dollar amount difference between what it pays and the cost of your premium is deposited it into your MSA. You use the MSA money to pay your medical expenses until your high deductible is reached. If the MSA money runs out, you pay out of your pocket until you reach the deductible. Any unused funds roll over to next year.

All of the above may not be available in your area.

years, there will only be certain times during the year that you can make such a switch, but you will be free to do so if you wish. Keep in mind that if you want to enroll in traditional fee-for-service insurance, **you may not be automatically eligible for a Medigap policy.**

Under the new law, if you leave your HMO within the first twelve months of initially selecting a Medicare HMO option or if you move out of your health plan's service area, Medigap insurers cannot deny your application. This is the case as long as you remember to apply within 63 days of leaving your HMO. If you have exercised the Medicare HMO option for longer than a year and then decide to switch to traditional Part B Medicare or if you delay in applying, the possibility of obtaining a Medigap policy can be reduced, particularly if you have health problems. It is important to **test your HMO** once you do enroll to be sure it is right for you.

A last concern involving HMOs is that they operate within a defined service area. For most people, this will not be a problem. But for those with children in college, who travel a lot or who regularly take extended vacations away from home, this can be a concern. HMOs are required to cover emergency care costs wherever they occur, but they do not have to pay for routine care outside of their service area. If you expect to spend a lot of time away from home, check with the HMO of your choice to see if they have reciprocal care arrangements with an HMO in the area in which you will be spending substantial time. If you remain in the service area, traditional Medicare fee-for-service or one of the new Medicare+Choice options may be better for you. If you now have Medicare, you can keep your present coverage. Most people do.

CONSUMER PROTECTIONS

New statutory provisions:

❑ Medicare+Choice plans must provide for patient confidentiality by safeguarding beneficiaries' health information.

- Unrestricted communication between patients and health care professionals is required. Gag clauses are prohibited.
- Medicare+Choice plans must cover care that a "prudent lay person" would consider an emergency, even if it proves to be a "false alarm."
- Medicare+Choice plans must make medical care and advice available on a 24-hour-per-day, 7-day-per-week basis.
- Out of area dialysis must be covered during an enrollee's temporary absence from the service area.
- Copayments for emergency services shall be no more than $50.
- The decision of the examining physician treating the individual enrollee prevails in consideration for discharge or transfer. (codification of existing policy)
- Women enrollees may choose direct access to a women's health specialist within the network for women's routine and preventive health (CBRR).
- Procedures must be approved by the Health Care Financing Administration for individuals with complex or serious medical conditions. These procedures include identification, assessment, development of an appropriate treatment plan, and the right to direct access to specialist (CBRR). Services must be provided in a culturally competent manner i.e. with sensitivity towards cultural, ethnic and language differences (CBRR).

MANAGE YOUR HEALTH CARE

When you have a medical problem, learn all you can about it, whatever your health coverage. Check your library, the internet, the organization that focuses on that particular medical problem (The American Cancer Society etc.). Get a second opinion from a specialist. Your local hospital will suggest names of specialists(you may have to pay). Then politely question your doctor or HMO. Insist on answers.

FREE MEDICARE & RELATED PUBLICATIONS

- Does Your Doctor or Supplier Accept Assignment?
- Guide to Choosing a Nursing Home
- Guide to Health Insurance for People With Medicare
- Health Plan Comparison Information
- Learning About Medicare Health Plans
- Medicare Coverage of Kidney Dialysis and Kidney Transplant Services
- Medicare Health Plan Quality and Satisfaction Information
- Medicare Home Health Care Services
- Medicare Hospice Benefits
- Medicare Preventive Services
- Medicare Supplemental Insurance (Medigap) Policies and Protections
- Medicare & You (Available in English, Spanish, Audio-tape or Braille)
- Worksheet for Comparing Medicare Health Plans
- Your Guide to Medicare Medical Savings Accounts
- Your Guide to Private Fee-for-Service Plan

For the above free publications call Medicare:

800-MEDICARE (800-633-4227)
www.medicare.gov

* * *

- A Shoppers Guide to Long-Term Care Insurance

For this free publication write to:

NAIC, Publications Dept.
120 West 12th Street, Suite 1100
Kansas City, MO 64105

STEPS FOR AN APPEAL

Members of HMOs who feel their denial of specialist care is unwarranted can appeal the decision. Thousands every year do, and win approximately 35% of the time, but it takes tenacity.

Steps to take:

- ❏ Find out which health plan employee made the initial denial and what grounds were cited.
- ❏ Ask your doctor to support your appeal.
- ❏ Call the HMO's hot line or member service department promptly to get an appeal started.
- ❏ If your appeal is turned down, ask for a rehearing at a higher level within the plan or appeal to state regulators. If you are a Medicare member, you have federal appeal rights. Ask for a reconsideration request.
- ❏ **Document everything.**
- ❏ See whether your health plan will provide a reasonable compromise.
- ❏ Find out if an advocacy group or government agency can help you. Your local Office on Aging can assist you.
- ❏ Be strong willed but civil. Even though you may be upset, you can get your point across better by being courteous and rational.
- ❏ If your medical condition requires prompt attention, pay the bill yourself under protest. Then proceed with your appeal.

- ❏ What kind of problems are you likely to face? That information is set out in a new National Association of Insurance Commissioners Action Kit, *"Resolving Health Insurance Complaints"* which is available free from your state insurance department.

IMPORTANT NOTE

As a result of complaints, steps have been taken by the Federal Government, State Insurance Departments, and the Courts to change procedures that may result in unsatisfactory care.

The HCFA has set new timeliness standards for appeal rights of Medicare beneficiaries:

- ❏ Appeals procedures will be expedited in cases in which a delay could endanger a beneficiary's health.
- ❏ Under the Medicare+Choice regulations, time frames are shortened.
- ❏ First level determination is to be made by the Medicare+Choice organization within 4 days.
- ❏ A reconsideration decision by the organization or the review entity is to be made within 30 days.
- ❏ For expedited appeals, a decision must be rendered within 72 hours.

Stay tuned. Your Medicare Hotline number will be helpful (800-638-6833 or www.medicare.gov) as will your local Agency on Aging.

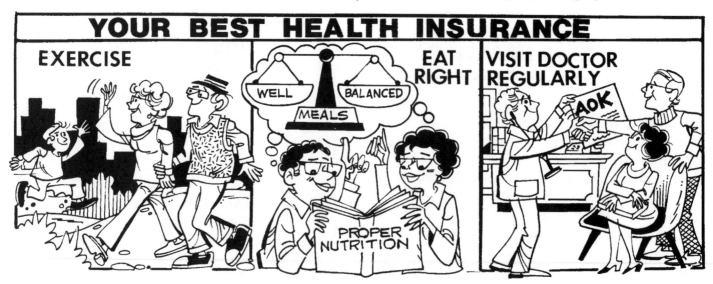

WHERE WILL YOU LIVE?

Where shall we live when we're retired?

Should we move or stay here?

If we move, where should we go?

Those are probably the most discussed questions when husbands and wives begin looking ahead to settling down into retirement life. They are very serious questions: The right decision could determine how comfortable, happy and secure retirement will be.

Americans are the most mobile people in the civilized world. Moving is a way of life because of job changes and transfers. Studies have shown that the average American changes homes every four years, usually within the same community, but frequently into homes in other cities and states.

This mobility results in families and friends scattered around the country—brothers and sisters in Virginia, a daughter in New England, another daughter in Washington state and a son still at home with soon-to-retire parents in New Jersey.

The wide separation of families and friends is in sharp contrast to well-rooted, close-knit families and communities abroad. Perhaps seeking to restart ties, as retirement approaches, many Americans consider moving closer to children, grandchildren, other relatives, or good friends who have moved away.

But should you?

There are many factors to be considered in addition to a natural desire to be closer to family and friends. It's not enough to say, "It'd be good to be nearer the kids."

Remember this: Their way of life may not be yours; their friends might not become your friends, if they should decide to seek better job opportunities elsewhere, you might be left behind, lonelier than ever.

Start thinking early about where you would be happiest in retirement, and remember, where you live in retirement will be a critical factor in what you do for the extra income you might need, for personal relationships, for leisure activities, for health and comfort, etc. Explore all your options.

It is not too early to think about all of this, even if retirement is still 10 years in the future.

There are a number of options available. What you choose will depend upon your own circumstances, needs and preferences. Your health

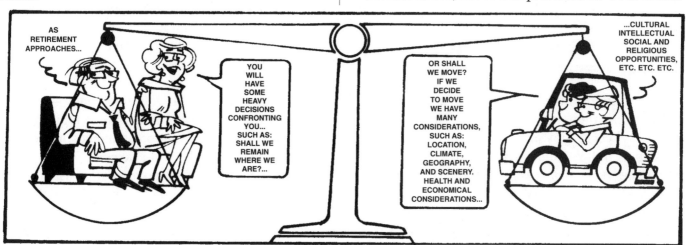

may dictate that you should move to a milder climate. Your plans for leisure activities may make you move closer to nature, or keep you close to the cultural offerings of the larger cities.

WHAT'S IMPORTANT TO YOU?

- ❏ Climate
- ❏ Distance from family
- ❏ Cost of moving
- ❏ Transportation facilities available
- ❏ Police and fire protection
- ❏ Cultural and intellectual offerings
- ❏ Shopping facilities nearby
- ❏ Taxes
- ❏ Place of worship nearby
- ❏ Physical limitations of family members
- ❏ Types of recreational facilities available
- ❏ Availability of employment
- ❏ Cost
- ❏ Safety of neighborhood
- ❏ Individual preference regarding isolation
- ❏ Good hospital nearby

A booklet, *Staying at Home: A Guide to Long Term Care and Housing,* discusses the types of housing and care that are available nationwide. For a free copy, write to: AARP, Fulfillment, 601 E Street, NW, Washington, DC 20049. Ask for publication D14986.

MOVING IS APPEALING, BUT...

The majority of those retiring say that they have given "some thought" to relocating. However, most stay where they are.

Studies indicate that only 20% to 25% of those who retire move away from their home communities within the first few years of retirement. Most who do move stay in the same state. Perhaps no more than 5% move to other states and other parts of the country.

Of the 75% to 80% who remain in their home communities, a substantial number do move to smaller homes or apartments, or to other neighborhoods.

Despite all the advertising lures to "the rich possibilities for long healthy, rewarding retirement" in Sunbelt communities, the majority of retirees are not pulling up their deep roots to move away.

Certainly, Florida is full of retirees. So are Arizona and other areas away from snow and cold. So is North Carolina, an "in" state for many retiring today. Still, the numbers moving into Sunbelt—or Retirement Belt—states are a relatively low percentage of those retiring.

...MOST STAY PUT

Why do most people stay where they are? It's not simply inertia. Many are too closely tied to homes to move away. They value the memories. They want to remain near friends and neighbors, to stay in their churches, clubs and organizations with people they know, to do business with banks and stores they are accustomed to. In a nutshell, they want to continue living as much as possible as they did before retirement.

In thinking about where you will live in retirement, it is a good idea to begin by thinking about where you are living now. Why did you choose your present home? What are its advantages? Its disadvantages?

Did you make sacrifices in order to be convenient to your job or, perhaps, your spouse's job? To be near schools, no longer an advantage now that children are grown? To have space you no longer need, or perhaps a larger yard for the children?

Think, also, of what you might gain—or give up—by moving into a smaller home requiring less care, inside and outdoors, and costing less for utilities and perhaps for taxes.

Another option is to move to an assisted living community, in which you live independently but that provides support such as light housekeeping or daily meals. Some communities may have nursing care for residents who become ill.

CHECKLIST FOR LIVING

(Yes) (No)

❑ ❑ Is my present house suitable for retirement living?

❑ ❑ Can my present house be remodeled for satisfactory retirement living?

❑ ❑ Will I be able to handle the upkeep and maintenance of the house?

❑ ❑ Will the costs of taxes and insurance be in my budget?

❑ ❑ Can my house be converted to a two-family house to rent?

❑ ❑ Have I checked the zoning?

❑ ❑ Have I considered using my home equity for income?

❑ ❑ Is my present neighborhood safe?

❑ ❑ Have I checked the security of my house?

❑ ❑ Have I planned how to spend my time?

❑ ❑ Am I active in my community?

❑ ❑ Are my friends important to me?

❑ ❑ Is it important to be near my family?

❑ ❑ Do I want to keep working after I retire?

❑ ❑ Do I want to stay where I'm known?

❑ ❑ Do I want to make a fresh start somewhere else?

❑ ❑ Before I move to a new area, have I experienced its different seasons?

❑ ❑ Is it close to shopping and public transportation?

❑ ❑ Is it near good medical care?

Be very careful—get legal and financial advice

RELOCATION CONSIDERATIONS

If you have considered staying in your present community and decided against it, go slow about making a final commitment.

A decision to relocate is, almost invariably, irreversible. Moving is physically and psychologically difficult—and it is an expensive drain on retirement resources.

Be absolutely sure of whatever decision you make. Here are some things to consider:

❑ **Climate, geography and scenery.** No place offers a perfect year-round climate: Florida's promised winter warmth turns into hot and humid discomfort. If you enjoy the changing seasons, the sameness of Florida's climate will very quickly pall. If you're accustomed to mountains, hills and rolling country, the flatness in plains states will make you homesick. It's a good idea to visit a location you're interested in at different times of the year—and stay long enough to recognize the flaws along with the advantages.

❑ **Health advantages and facilities.** Many retirees who decide to relocate do so for health reasons. Respiratory, coronary and rheumatic conditions might be relieved by settling in the right place—or can be aggravated by a wrong choice. Don't make a decision to relocate without consulting your doctor. And check on the availability of doctors and hospitals or clinics, wherever you go. Don't take for granted that emergency help will be available.

❑ **Economics.** Check the cost of living in any area in which you want to locate. It's a good idea to subscribe to a local newspaper and read it carefully to learn about prices (check the ads) and business activity. If you want to augment your income in retirement, are there job opportunities? Want ads might tell you, but you probably will have to check the Chamber of Commerce or a Senior Citizen Agency. Remember, if you save money on clothing, heating and housing costs in Sunbelt areas, the savings may be partially offset by air conditioning costs during most of the year.

❑ **Religious and social opportunities.** Make sure that you can continue to enjoy the kind of religious and social life you have had before. Are the facilities available? Generally, they are, almost everywhere, but be sure to check. The same advice goes for recreational and sports possibilities, and for hobbies. The friendship you find in religious, social, recreational, sports and hobby groups is important to your happiness in a new home.

❑ **Cultural and intellectual advantages.** Many communities that are desirable places to live are limited in cultural and intellectual opportunities. You might not be able to take continuing education courses, enter Great Books discussion groups, enjoy good live performances of plays, music or the dance, or browse through museums. If these are things you enjoy, perhaps you'd better look for a college town offering these and all the other advantages you're seeking in a retirement home.

❑ **Location and accessibility.** Shopping centers, restaurants, libraries, theaters, post offices, and other everyday facilities you might want are easily accessible almost everywhere now. Certainly you'll have no problems if you have a car. Still, check. Also, don't forget to look into the accessibility of airports offering adequate flight service. And is there train service? What about buses?

❑ **Personal relationships.** If you have no friends or relatives in the place you'd like to make your retirement home, visit enough times to be sure the residents are congenial. Almost always they will be, but "outsiders" find it hard to break through barriers in a few places. The lack of quick friendliness and total acceptance in a community creates additional strain at a time when tearing up roots in one place and trying to set them in another is traumatic enough.

Briefly: organize your thinking when you consider moving. Decide what you want and need in a new home, check carefully rather than deciding on a basis of retirement community ads or sunshine when you've just left winter snow, and visit at different times of the year. Summer vacations could be a start, but take time off later to sample other seasons. Be over-cautious rather than sorry when it's too late.

There is a good test of how happy and well adjusted a retiree will be in a new retirement home.

How happy are you in your present community?

If you are happy, active, a part of the community, enjoying its advantages and helping to serve its needs, there is almost no doubt that you can be as happy and adjusted in a new community.

If you have never become a part of your community, arguing that you are too busy and just not interested, don't expect changes if you relocate.

When you go into a new community aggressively, don't wait to be invited to church, service or other clubs, or to participate in activities generally. Introduce yourself, mention what you were interested in before and say, "I'd like to be a part of things here."

You won't lack friends or a busy and useful life.

If you decide to relocate, the success of your move in the long run will be up to you.

THE 1997 FEDERAL TAX LAW
SALE OF YOUR HOME

Excludes from tax the profits on home or apartment sales up to $250,000 for singles and $500,000 for couples, irrespective of age (applicable to sales after May 6, 1997). The exclusion can be used more than once. The home or apartment must be the primary residence of at least one spouse for at least two of the past five years.

LIVE WITH RELATIVES

Health factors may combine with economic ones to make living with children a necessity. The need for privacy suggests that even in these conditions, measures should be taken to avoid the unnecessary stress that can occur when two independent family units are forced into close association. It will require tact, maturity, and considerable caring on the part of family members to survive such forced intimacy without a deterioration of relationships.

There should be an understanding about roles in the family, and the older members of the household should share in the responsibilities of running the home. They should be given something constructive to do.

Where possible, private living room, bedroom, and bath facilities will enable the individual to have an independence important to self-respect. Efforts should be made to encourage the family member to maintain a schedule of activities independent of the activities of the family. Interests and friendships should be cultivated apart from the home.

KEEP UP TO DATE

CHECKLIST FOR SAFETY

(Yes) (No)

❑ ❑ No-slip tape in your bathtub or shower?

❑ ❑ Grab bars and hand grips in shower, bathtubs and near toilets?

❑ ❑ Can your towel bars and soap holders withstand sudden pulls?

❑ ❑ Keep throw rugs away from top and bottom of stairs?

❑ ❑ Do all rugs have no-slip mats under them?

❑ ❑ Do not wear loose-fitting slippers or bathrobes?

❑ ❑ Are all chairs and stairs sturdy and free of wobbles?

❑ ❑ Replace all frayed cords and broken plugs?

❑ ❑ Relocate all furniture, lamp cords and clutter from traffic paths?

❑ ❑ Do not run extension cords under rugs or carpets?

❑ ❑ Avoid using space heaters, if possible. If they are necessary, keep away from flammable materials and out of traffic lanes?

❑ ❑ No smoking while lying down?

❑ ❑ Install smoke detectors and heat detectors throughout the house?

❑ ❑ Install fire extinguishers near kitchen and work room?

❑ ❑ Have escape routes planned from all areas of home in case of fire?

❑ ❑ Avoid overloading one socket with several plugs?

❑ ❑ Discard heavy, hard to handle, broken cooking utensils?

❑ ❑ Are there handrails on all stairs and inclines?

❑ ❑ Install night lights in the bedroom, bathroom and hallways?

❑ ❑ Make sure stairways and other areas are well lighted?

❑ ❑ If you live alone, have a friend or relative check in with you at regular intervals?

❑ ❑ Keep first aid kit handy. Take first aid course, CPR course. Place emergency phone numbers near phone?

EARN MONEY IN RETIREMENT

"Growing old is no more than a bad habit which a busy man has no time to learn." **ANDRE MAUROIS**

Do you have to work after retirement? Many people who could answer "no" to this question from a purely economic point of view, would have to say "yes" from a psychological one. There are other compulsions than not having enough income to live comfortably. Some people must work because of the additional rewards which work affords. Some must work to have an identity.

"What do you do?" is translated by some into the question, **"Who are you?"** Not having a job is almost like not being anybody. "I am what I do." We have looked at this problem in our discussion about leisure. You are *more* than your job, but some people find in employment the activity which keeps them from learning the "bad habit" of growing old. (To work and receive Social Security see Chapter 3.)

MUST I? MAY I?

The question for many is decided in terms of economic necessity. Work is essential for adequate income. The other question is, given that I wish to work, will I be able to find a job? Who will be interested in having an individual who has been retired from active work? "How can I compete with the younger worker in terms of strength, ability to learn, contribution to the company?"

Given a choice, most older workers would prefer continuing with some kind of employment. Work makes a contribution to our lives which is not easily replaced by anything else. What, other than work, can give the following satisfactions to life?

- ❑ It is the basis for self-respect, for feeling that you are somebody who has something to contribute.
- ❑ It is a source of prestige and recognition. People appreciate your ability to perform.
- ❑ It provides a place for social participation. How many of your friendships are related to the job?
- ❑ It is a source of enjoyment, a chance to be creative.
- ❑ It is a way of helping others.
- ❑ It helps give order to the day, making time pass. You don't have to plan for, or organize a great part of the day.

THE ENEMY IS US

The greatest obstacle to finding employment may be the attitude which you have about yourself. To turn a familiar phrase, "we have nothing to fear but fear itself."

It's true that there are a number of misconceptions about older workers. But there are some strengths which mature workers have. Focus on the positive things which you have to offer.

CHANGES IN THE LAW THAT WILL AFFECT YOU!

END OF MANDATORY RETIREMENT AT AGE 70

WE CAN WORK... ...AS LONG AS WE LIKE!

The Department of Labor and other agencies have studied the performance of older workers and have come up with the following facts that refute the myths about older workers:

Myth: "Older workers are too slow. They can't meet production requirements."

❑ *Fact:* There is no significant drop in performance and productivity. In fact, many older workers exceed the average output of younger employees.

Myth: "Older workers can't meet the physical demands of jobs."

❑ *Fact:* Only fourteen percent of today's jobs require great strength and heavy lifting. Labor-saving machinery makes it possible for older workers to handle eighty-six percent of modern jobs without difficulty.

Myth: "Older workers are absent too often."

❑ *Fact:* The attendance of workers over 65 compares favorably with other age groups.

Myth: "Older workers are inflexible. They're hard to train because they can't accept change."

❑ *Fact:* Adaptability depends on the individual, not on his age. Some young people are set in their ways, while a high proportion of older workers show flexibility in accepting a change in occupation and earnings.

Myth: "Hiring older workers increases our pensions and insurance costs."

❑ *Fact:* Most pension plans provide for benefits related to length of service, earnings, or both. Small, additional pensions, when incurred, are more than offset by the worker's experience, lower turnover, and quality of work. The costs of group life, accident, and health insurance and workmen's compensation are *not* materially increased by hiring older workers.

The following check list contains favorable and unfavorable attitudes of older workers. Which ones apply to you?

❑ Defeatist attitude toward getting work and difficult time impressing an employer favorably.

❑ Stability which comes with maturity.

❑ Wastes less time on job than younger worker.

❑ Feels he is slowing down, and talks about this feeling with prospective employer.

❑ Forgotten how to go about getting a job.

❑ Less absenteeism; more apt to stay on the job.

❑ Safe work habits.

❑ Reluctant to change occupations even though there is no work available in line with previous work.

❑ Refuses to consider jobs paying less or having less prestige than former jobs because of personal pride.

❑ Difficulty making a realistic evaluation of limitations. Makes unrealistic demands as to wages, location, working conditions, etc.

❑ Greater sense of responsibility.

❑ Steady work habits and serious attitude.

❑ Good appearance.

❑ Requires less supervision, once trained.

❑ Tends to undersell self and fails to impress prospective employers favorably.

❑ Less distracted by outside interests, has fewer domestic troubles, and is capable of greater concentration.

AMERICANS AT WORK

Age group	Percentage of men employed full-time	Percentage of women employed full-time	Age group	Percentage of men employed full- or part-time	Percentage of women employed full- or part-time
45 to 54	82.8	47.2	60 and 61	65.7	38.6
55 to 59	71.0	35.3	62 to 64	44.3	27.7
60 to 64	46.1	21.7	65 to 69	23.6	13.0
65 and older	8.2	2.7	70 and older	10.3	4.2

IF YOU HAD YOUR DRUTHERS...

If you had the job of matching the interests, skills, experience, and situation of a person like yourself to a job, what kind of employment would you select? Maybe you need to look at all of these factors to get a total picture. You may be interested in doing something for which you have little experience. You may not like the kind of work in which you have experience. Try "brainstorming"

with your answers to the following questions:

Past Jobs Held
What did you like and dislike?

Skills and Abilities
What can you do best?

Educational Qualifications
Have you had special instruction?

Physical Limitations
Does your health rule out some jobs?

Goals
What would be ideal for you?

YOUR EXPERIENCE INVENTORY

EMPLOYMENT OBJECTIVE (As clearly and concisely as possible, indicate what you want to do)

_____

_____

EMPLOYMENT HISTORY (List employment in reverse chronological order)

Dates: From-To	Job Title & Responsibilities	Company Name & Location
_____	_____	_____
_____	_____	_____
_____	_____	_____
_____	_____	_____

MISCELLANEOUS EMPLOYMENT (List part-time and/or minor employments, if these would help)

_____

EDUCATION (List schools in reverse chronological order)

Dates: From-To	Name of School & Location	Degree/Last Grade Completed
_____	_____	_____
_____	_____	_____

ADDITIONAL EDUCATION (List correspondence schools, company courses, seminars, etc.)

_____

_____

PROFESSIONAL ASSOCIATIONS (List organizations to which you belong or did belong)

_____

_____

INTERESTS (List hobbies or volunteer activities, especially if they relate to the job you want)

_____

_____

THE JOB INTERVIEW

If you decide that you want to work for somebody else, you will usually have to talk to a representative of that company before you are employed. In the job interview you have a few minutes to tell about your qualifications. You will likely be talking to someone younger than yourself. The job may pay less than what you earned before retirement. Are you confident enough about yourself to avoid feeling defensive? Can you discuss your skills and experience realistically? Can you face the prospect of not receiving a job without feeling rejected as a person?

However you answer the preceding questions, you will find the interview more likely to result in a favorable impression of you if you:

❑ Stress your skills, not your limitations.

❑ Are poised and confident, but not cocky.

❑ Are pleasant, but business-like.

❑ Speak firmly and clearly.

❑ Listen attentively to your interviewer's questions.

❑ Answer briefly and honestly.

❑ Stress your stability and good attendance record.

❑ Ask intelligent questions about the nature of the job.

❑ Are realistic about your salary requirements.

❑ Leave when the interview is over, thanking the employer for the opportunity.

HOW NOT TO IMPRESS

Poor impressions are left by those who…

❑ Are timid and ill at ease.

❑ Are stubborn and argumentative.

❑ Stress their need for a job.

❑ Emphasize their age or personal problems.

❑ Exaggerate their skills.

❑ Criticize a former employer.

❑ Talk too long.

❑ Discuss salary, benefits, and hours *before* the employer brings up the subjects.

❑ Show reluctance: to fill out an application form, give references, or take a physical exam if requested.

JOB SEARCH SOURCES

There are sources of help in locating a job or developing the skills needed to get one.
They are:

❑ Friends, relatives, former co-workers, or members of your social group can be helpful. Tell them that you're looking for a job; and ask them for help in finding one.

❑ Want ads in newspapers, professional journals, and trade magazines.

❑ Industrial and craft unions.

- Private employment agencies (some charge the applicant a fee, and others collect the fee from the employer).
- Yellow pages of telephone directory, industrial directories, Chamber of Commerce lists.
- Professional associations.
- Forty-Plus Clubs for executives in major cities.
- Retired Officers Association (for members) 201 N. Washington St. Alexandria, VA 22314-2539.
- Personnel offices.
- College placement offices.
- The library.
- Nonprofit employment agencies. Your local Chamber of Commerce, and YMCA, Salvation Army, and your state employment agency should be able to tell you if there are agencies in your area.

SECOND CAREERS

In today's job market, with down-sizing, early retirement, and company mergers, many find themselves looking for a new job or a new career at a relatively early age. This is a marked change from the employment stability many enjoyed ten and twenty years ago. Millions of Americans have been and will be affected by this change.

What to do? While still working, continually develop your skills, either at work, at your local adult educational center, community college, or university. Take courses that interest you and in subject areas where job possibilities could develop.

There are positive factors. You have work skills and experience. Older workers are needed almost everywhere.

- Take an inventory of your talents.
- List your goals, what you've always wanted to do, what you would enjoy doing.
- Where are your skills needed?
- Volunteering can open job possibilities.

Note: Over 75% of all jobs are never listed in newspapers or public employment agencies.

WORK FOR YOURSELF–OR OTHERS

If you want to have a good job interview with a person you really like, and have your resume read by admiring and sympathetic eyes, try making an application to *yourself* for a job! You can work out the hours which are agreeable to employer and employee, and there will never be a discussion over wages. Some retired persons will want to consider being their own boss, and there are many ways that this can be done.

WHAT A WORKER OVER AGE 65 IN 2000 NETS FROM A JOB

Employment Income (Annual)	$20,000.00	$30,000.00	$40,000.00
Reduction in Social Security benefits	1,000.00	4,333.00	7,666.00
Social Security tax (FICA)	1,530.00	2,295.00	3,060.00
Additional federal/state taxes (*estimated*)	3,000.00	4,500.00	6,000.00
Job expenses (travel, lunch, etc.) (*estimated*)	3,000.00	3,000.00	3,000.00
Net Earnings	**11,470.00**	**15,872.00**	**20,274.00**
Monthly (Net) Earnings	**955.83**	**1,322.66**	**1,689.50**

Note: You may earn up to $17,000 per year in 2000 without losing any Social Security benefits. Starting at age 70, you may earn an unlimited amount and not lose benefits.

WORKING FOR YOURSELF

Operating a part-time business may be your answer to the need to supplement your income and find meaningful ways to invest your time. If it is done on a small scale, it may not require as much capital and know-how as you would imagine.

Considerable caution should be exercised, however, in the selection of a business. On average your chances of remaining three years in your business are about 50-50. A Dun and Bradstreet survey revealed that 90% of such business failures were due to inexperience.

This is the age of the chain and the corporation. Your choice of a business should not lead you into competition with such tough competitors.

Check a regional office of the Small Business Administration for advice and information about opening a business, via the internet: www.sba.gov or write to:

Small Business Administration
 409 3rd Street, SW,
Washington, DC 20416.

Try to get an early start preparing for the business you will operate in retirement. You will need time to familiarize yourself with the business, accumulate the capital needed for the investment, and purchase equipment needed *before* attempting to live on a retirement budget.

CHOOSING YOUR BUSINESS

Answering the questions listed below should give you some insights into the type of business which best suits you.

- ❑ How well do I get along with other people?
- ❑ Am I ready to assume responsibility for payroll and business obligations?
- ❑ Do I like the proposed business enough to sacrifice for it?

- ❑ Am I prepared to take the risk involved in owning a business?
- ❑ Do I like to sell?
- ❑ Can I make decisions and live with them?
- ❑ How do I react to emergencies?
- ❑ Am I a good organizer?

The U.S. Small Business Administration lists 10 characteristics that a businessman should have.

Rank yourself from 1 (exceptional), 2 (above average), 3 (average), 4 (below average), to 5 (deficient) to find your business potential.

Trait	Rank
Initiative	_____
Positive attitude	_____
Leadership ability	_____
Organizing ability	_____
Industry	_____
Responsibility	_____
Quick and accurate judgments	_____
Sincerity	_____
Perseverance	_____
High level of energy	_____

The more "1's" and "2's" you have listed, the easier it will be for you to adjust to running a business.

Considering the high mortality rate of business, and the possibilities of over-extending yourself in demands on your money, health and time, get plenty of information, and be sure that you know what you need in going into business.

WORKING AT HOME

Having your business where you live—more than 40 million Americans work out of their homes— eliminates some of the problems of working at a separate location. You do not have to worry about paying rent for the business, nor do you have to incur transportation costs getting to and from work.

It will also be easier to maintain a schedule that is more relaxed if you are working out of your own home.

One warning, though: Check out any zoning regulations or licensing procedures that you might have to comply with, that apply to businesses in private homes. Be sure you're covered by adequate insurance.

FRANCHISES

This is the kind of business venture which has some of the features of owning your own business and some of the features of working for somebody else. You have to put up some capital, but often the national organization has standards and methods of operation which are part of your obligation to the jointly-owned business. The organization often will assume responsibility for giving you training, and will supervise the market so that no unfair competition will arise from another member of the same organization.

Franchises are really a form of licensing. The franchisor, which is usually an owner of a service, product or method, distributes through affiliated dealers who are the franchises. If you purchase a franchise, often you will be given exclusive rights to the area served by your franchise. But you can still run into trouble from other companies offering similar franchises, so be careful to check beforehand for competition in your area.

A franchise should be carefully investigated before the decision is made to invest in it. Many fraudulent promoters are at work in the field, offering schemes which are little more than obligations on the part of the "victims" to purchase

THE BUSINESS PLAN: ITS USES

If you wish to start your own business, preparing a good business plan is the first step. If you need financing, or want to bring your bank manager on board in case you run into problems, you'll need a business plan. Having a thorough one demonstrates that you are a self-starter who has put a great deal of thought into your business idea.

Aside from money matters, a business plan will help your overall management of your new enterprise. Getting the business plan right can mean the difference between success and failure.

What does a good business plan look like? Each business plan is different, but, in general, it should include a description of the business, including short- and long-term goals, an analysis of the market being entered (including a discussion of competitors' strengths and weaknesses and your competitive advantage), and financial details including start-up costs, the size of the investment required and profit and cash-flow projections for a minimum of one year ahead.

supplies or goods from the promoters.

Good advice is available from Better Business Bureau, Chambers of Commerce, and others, so that no individual need stumble into a venture without adequate information.

WHEN CONSIDERING A SECOND CAREER...

| 1-KNOW WHAT YOU WANT FROM YOUR NEW CAREER | 2-TAKE INVENTORY OF YOUR TALENTS AND DREAMS | 3-ENJOY EXPLORING 2nd CAREER OPTIONS | 4-LEARN A NEW CAREER, JOB OR SKILL | 5-HOW ABOUT STARTING YOUR OWN BUSINESS |

WORKING FOR OTHERS

Look at Chapter 11, on volunteering, to share your time with others. There are jobs which are directly related to service for others, and the compensation is a combination of a modest pay check and the knowledge that you have made life more rewarding for someone else. These jobs take as much of your time as you care to give.

BE PREPARED

If you are seriously interested in developing the skills necessary to go back to work or start your own business, two of the best places to go for information and help are your public library and your local college.

Library shelves usually have sections on Employment and Retirement, either category might have the facts and advice you're looking for.

Colleges, particularly Junior and Community Colleges, also provide services for job seekers. In addition to courses which can develop skills and expertise in specific areas (such as Business, Accounting, or Education), many colleges offer classes designed for adults who wish to know more about developing second careers and getting back into the employment mainstream. Check with your local two-year college for program details.

BOOKS THAT CAN HELP

The author Richard Bolles has written two books that have successfully guided job seekers over the years.

The Quick Job-Hunting Map. Richard Bolles. 1997. ISBN# 1-89815-387-5. $4.95 plus $4.50 handling.

What Color Is Your Parachute & Practical Manual for Job Hunters & Career Changers. Richard Bolles. 2000. ISBN# 1-58008-123-1. $16.95 plus $4.50 handling.

You can order these books from:
Ten Speed Press
P.O. Box 7123
Berkeley, CA 94707.
www.tenspeed.com

MYTH

"A perpetual holiday is a good working definition of hell." —GEORGE BERNARD SHAW

"All animals except man know that the chief business of life is to enjoy it."—SAMUEL BUTLER

"Success or failure in the second forty years, measured in terms of happiness, is determined more by how we use or abuse our leisure than any other factor ... a super abundance of leisure, or the abuse thereof has marked and initiated the decadence of cultures throughout history." —DR. EDWARD J. STIEGLITZ

❑ Will your leisure be the perpetual holiday mentioned by Shaw, or the time when you discover how to enjoy life as never before?

❑ Will your use of leisure time result in success or failure in your attempt to achieve happiness during retirement?

❑ How much leisure time will you have on your hands, and how difficult will your schedule be after full-time employment no longer accounts for the major part of your daytime activities? What will replace the satisfaction that work has afforded?

Answering the above questions will lead you into an examination of yourself...who you really are...what you really want...what your attitude is toward the use of your time. This chapter will provide you with an opportunity to look at yourself and to consider the alternatives available for structuring your time.

You'll explore what adjustments may be necessary to meet your basic needs, as you attempt to fill your life with meaning that is not derived specifically from the "work ethic."

Retirement should be a transition from toil to leisure. It should see a transfer of the energies you formerly devoted to making a living, to the *new business* of living well. In the transition, you will learn to reallocate your time.

As you look toward having "nothing to do," it seems very appealing after so many years of having too little "free time." If you look forward to "doing nothing," plan to do a lot of that...for a few weeks. Fishing?... traveling?... just sitting in the rocking chair?... Yes, all of those things... for a short time.

VACATION: EACH DAY OF THE YEAR

Remember, however, that the reason doing nothing seems so appealing is because you have had little idle time. A vacation *is* a vacation because it comes infrequently, but a vacation *every day of the year*? That's something else again. Remember to build *quality* into your leisure hours.

Unplanned time leads to boredom, a feeling of guilt, and a sense of frustration. As strange as it may seem, many people prefer to work even when it is not an economic necessity.

CAN WORK BE MORE FUN?

A recent study at Duke University's Center on Aging revealed that over half of the 200 men surveyed (52%) said they got more satisfaction from *work* than they did from *leisure*. Fifty-five percent of the 200 women surveyed said they enjoyed working more than they did having free time.

"HAVE YOU CONSIDERED **REPAIRMAN**?"

CAN YOU ACCEPT LEISURE?

You need to decide whether or not you can accept the free time you have earned for yourself. We can be misers with our time or we can learn to use time generously.

We have had little preparation for leisure. Walter Kerr, in *The Decline of Pleasure*, notes that, "The twentieth century has relieved us of much labor without at the same time relieving us of the conviction that only labor is meaningful."

It may be, that to really enjoy leisure, you will have to "learn not to work." You may have to teach yourself that it is *right* for you to enjoy doing something for the pleasure it brings, without having to prove that it serves any higher purpose. You may have to retrain your mind to accept that leisure is not "inactivity," and that non-work activities may be as necessary and "useful" as those for which we formerly received paychecks.

The goal in retirement is not just to fill your time, but to fill it in a meaningful way. "Free time" is what you have when *you* determine what you will do.

"Leisure" is the term we apply to those activities with which we fill our "free time." The kind of leisure which we will be able to "accept" has the following characteristics:

- ❑ We do it because we want to.
- ❑ We anticipate it with pleasure and remember it fondly.
- ❑ We may do it alone, or with others.
- ❑ We feel good about it, physically and mentally.
- ❑ It contributes to others, as well as to ourselves.
- ❑ We may do it for fun, or we may do it for profit.

The correct use of leisure can affect our health and our wealth. We can lose both if our bodies and our minds are wasted through inactivity, or in useless occupation.

An aging individual, by aimless living, can accelerate his deterioration as he grows older. The older the individual, the greater is the need for an all-absorbing motive, an interest in life. At 55 or 60 or 65, instead of receding from the useful stream of meaningful activities, he should establish new interests, or a second career. — **DR. EDWARD L. BORTZ**

Learn to enjoy leisure. Work if you wish, and be as active in your retirement as you care to be, but accept the fact that it's OK to enjoy many different activities, including the activity of doing nothing.

ADDING SPICE TO YOUR LIFE

What you do with your time should be more than being busy. Activity which neglects the personality and the person is like throwing a life buoy to a drowning person; it keeps his head above the water, but doesn't really rescue him.

Demand that your efforts be rewarded. Don't settle for filling time! Those activities which are worth your time should ...

- ❑ Create excitement.
- ❑ Stimulate your emotions to give you renewed zest.

MEETING YOUR NEEDS THROUGH LEISURE ACTIVITIES

There are some basic needs which remain constant throughout life, and many of these can be met through a wise selection of leisure activities. Look at some of these basic needs, and see how they compare to your present leisure activities? List alongside the corresponding 'need' the activity which you are presently engaged in which makes a contribution to that need. In the right-hand column, list additional activities which you would like to consider in the future to meet that need.

Need	Present Activities	Projected Activities
Recognition		
Entertainment		
Self-expression, creativity		
Participation, belonging		
Adventure, new experience		
Learning		
Security		
Physical fitness		
Contemplation		
Self-growth		
Usefulness		
Income		

- ❏ Be both physically and intellectually stimulating.

It's a good idea to have your spouse ponder the same categories—then compare your impressions, and see what things you have in common to explore together in retirement!

WHAT'S BEST FOR YOU?

If you like an activity, that is one good reason for considering it, but there are other factors to consider. Some activities which have brought satisfaction to others have been found to have these qualities:

- ❏ A beginner can attain a sense of accomplishment.
- ❏ Basic skills can be mastered readily.
- ❏ Real proficiency can come with practice.
- ❏ So many facets that it doesn't become tiresome.
- ❏ Within your budget.
- ❏ Enlarges a skill you already possess.
- ❏ Offers opportunity for self-development.
- ❏ Provides a change of pace from your routine.
- ❏ Can be practiced all year long.
- ❏ Represents a blend of several activities.
- ❏ Can be pursued in spite of some physical limitations.
- ❏ Puts you in touch with other people.
- ❏ Provides challenges to improve or grow or become more proficient in an area of interest.

LEISURE POSSIBILITIES CHECK LIST

- ☐ Acting
- ☐ Bicycling
- ☐ Boating
- ☐ Bowling
- ☐ Camping
- ☐ Charitable Activities
- ☐ Club
- ☐ Collecting
- ☐ Community Projects
- ☐ Cooking
- ☐ Crafts
- ☐ Dancing
- ☐ Elderhostel
- ☐ Enjoying Nature
- ☐ Entertaining
- ☐ Exercising
- ☐ Family Activities
- ☐ Family Outings
- ☐ Fishing
- ☐ Gardening
- ☐ Golf
- ☐ Ham Radio

- ☐ Investing
- ☐ Learning
- ☐ Little League
- ☐ Museums/Art Galleries
- ☐ Music
- ☐ Painting
- ☐ Part Time Work
- ☐ Photography
- ☐ Politics
- ☐ Reading
- ☐ Religion
- ☐ Repairing Things
- ☐ Scout Master
- ☐ Sewing
- ☐ Sport Events
- ☐ Swimming
- ☐ Take Courses
- ☐ Television
- ☐ Time to be Alone
- ☐ Walking
- ☐ Woodworking
- ☐ Writing

START ENJOYING YOUR FAVORITE ACTIVITIES NOW!

..IN EARLY MORNING TAKE A WALK

STAY IN TOUCH WITH YOUNGER PEOPLE

HIKING TRAIL

PLAN SOME ACTIVITIES WITH FRIENDS

GOLF

STEP ONE: HELP YOURSELF

"People who stay young do so because of an active interest that provides satisfaction through participation." — **DR. WILLIAM C. MENNINGER**

"Wherever a man turns, he can find someone who needs him. Even if it is a little thing, do something for which you get no pay but the privilege of doing it. For remember, you don't live in a world all your own. Your brothers are here, too." — **DR. ALBERT SCHWEITZER**

"All who would win joy, must share it; happiness was born a twin." — **BYRON**

In the preceding chapter we looked at the amount of time you are going to have during retirement and suggested some possible uses for it. We suggested that you take a good look at yourself, and fill your time with experiences which give you pleasure. Relax, have a good time.

In this chapter we ask you to do the same thing. You probably won't be able to find continual happiness thinking only about yourself.

The human spirit is too great to be content seeking the gratification of its own desires. Because of the sheer "fun" of sharing, many people feel a keen satisfaction in giving a part of themselves to community service activities.

Plan for meaningful uses of the free time you

will have in retirement. A lack of planned time can lead to boredom, a feeling of guilt and a sense of frustration. Devote part of your time to that which gives you personal pleasure: spend time with a hobby, sports, self-expression or creativity, the adventures of travel, further education or just the entertainment of watching television, reading and listening to music. You have *earned* the right to enjoy leisure as you want to spend it.

However, for your fullest satisfaction in retirement years, consider spending part of your free time in volunteer work *with* and *for* others. One in every four adults in the United States does some volunteer work each year. It might not be much, and it might not be for a long time, but volunteer work does involve a sharing of personal time and interests, and participation with others toward a common objective.

SERVICE INSTEAD OF SALARY

You may not have decided to enter retirement without paid employment, but to the extent that your job responsibilities have lessened, your need for meaningful activity increases. You may not have realized the degree to which your sense of personal worth has been related to your job. During your early and middle years you have a definite (at times almost overwhelming) sense of responsibility. You are needed by family; you contribute to society through your work.

Community service activities now offer you such job-related satisfactions as:

- ❏ The comradeship of congenial people.
- ❏ A chance for recognition.
- ❏ An opportunity to contribute to a useful goal.
- ❏ An opportunity to belong to a worthwhile group.

You need to give of yourself *more* than the service organizations need to have your help. The principal beneficiary of your service is *you*.

There is really no way of listing all the things people do or the time they spend doing them—no way, for example, to total the hours devoted on Sundays to church work, the volunteer work of preparing for and teaching Sunday School classes. However, a recent Conference Board survey of 3,800 upper-echelon managers and professionals who retired from major U.S. corporations between 1961 and 1976 found that 11% were doing volunteer work while holding retirement jobs for pay and another 22% were working strictly as volunteers.

The point is, there's a need—often a very serious need—for every man or woman to serve, somewhere, as a volunteer worker. The extent of participation is up to the volunteer. It can be as little as an hour a week. It can be much more. It can be a minimum of personal involvement, with only routine chores, or it can be deeply personal.

Dr. Allen G. Brailey, a Boston physician noted the vital role which service plays in assuming the place formerly occupied by the job or the family. "Do not retire from work; retire to more congenial work for the Community Fund, for the Red Cross, for the church or the schools, for the Scouts." Service to one's fellow man fills the need in the retired person which service to children and grandchildren formerly supplied.

**"GEORGE SAID HE'D LOVE TO BE A VOLUNTEER...
...BUT THERE'S NOT MUCH DEMAND FOR WHAT HE DOES BEST."**

WHAT SHARING DOES

If activities are carefully selected, they can make the following contributions, most of which relate to your personal well-being:

- ❑ Lessen the shock of disengagement from work.
- ❑ Delay senility.
- ❑ Stimulate the mind and body, reducing health problems.
- ❑ Combat the waste of human resources.
- ❑ Enrich the community through volunteer services.
- ❑ Give positive pleasure.

CHOOSING THE BEST ACTIVITY

There are so many needs, you can afford to choose among them to find the one which suits what you have to offer. Begin early...even before you retire; this will give you a chance to practice. Some companies encourage employees approaching retirement to devote time *before* actual retirement to community service. This permits a gradual transfer of interest and skills to a service-oriented job as formal employment draws to a close.

Ask yourself the following questions when considering how to invest your time:

- ❑ Is it something about which I care deeply?
- ❑ Does it require a skill I possess?
- ❑ Does it provide association with congenial people?
- ❑ Does it require time I am prepared to give?
- ❑ Do I enjoy fixing things (if that is required)?
- ❑ Do I enjoy creating things (if that is required)?
- ❑ Am I good at selling things (if that is required)?
- ❑ Does it involve working with people or things? (Which do I prefer?)

YOUR INTERESTS AND SKILLS

Identify the resources that you have. On the list below, check the things which you do well and would like to share.

- ❑ Bookkeeping skills
- ❑ Caring for children
- ❑ Caring for older people
- ❑ Carpentry
- ❑ Church interests
- ❑ Entertaining skills
- ❑ Cooking skills
- ❑ Growing things
- ❑ Human concern
- ❑ Hunting skills
- ❑ Knowledge of athletics
- ❑ Legal knowledge
- ❑ Library skills
- ❑ Meeting people
- ❑ Nursing training
- ❑ Organizing ability
- ❑ Playing a musical instrument
- ❑ Photography skills
- ❑ Political interests
- ❑ Selling ideas
- ❑ Speaking skills
- ❑ Supervisory skills
- ❑ Teaching skills
- ❑ Typing facility
- ❑ Visiting skills
- ❑ Working with the handicapped
- ❑ Writing experience

WHERE TO VOLUNTEER

Many communities have central bureaus acting as clearing houses for nonprofit agencies in need of volunteer help. Look in the telephone directory under VOLUNTEER; COMMUNITY–Community Chest, Community Service Council; EXTENSION SERVICE.

Your local library should also have listings of volunteer opportunities in the area.

Check with the social, civic and religious groups represented in your community. They will have projects and can refer you to additional agencies which would welcome your participation.

How about politics? Check with your local party representatives for suggestions about how you can support candidates and issues you respect. The League of Women Voters offers opportunities for women to be informed and influential in the political arena.

YOUR ASSETS: WHO NEEDS THEM

Nationwide, at least four and a half million persons age 65 or over are currently engaged in some type of volunteer work. If you are considering sharing your knowledge and experience through volunteer work, you can begin looking in your own neighborhood. Chances are, many groups in your area engage volunteer workers or are seeking their help.

After-school programs at your local school, church or synagogue, Salvation Army center or Y could be greatly expanded with your volunteer help. Many working parents are unable to be with their children until late in the afternoon. Volunteering to participate in constructive after-school programs benefits not only the children but yourself as well as you find an enjoyable and valuable way to contribute to the community.

Other ideas:
- ❑ Helping at your church or synagogue
- ❑ Collecting and repairing clothing
- ❑ Providing transportation to the aged for shopping and visits to the doctor
- ❑ Conducting parties at shut-in centers
- ❑ Making tray favors for hospital patients
- ❑ Assisting with public health programs
- ❑ Volunteering for work in nursing homes
- ❑ Participating in telephone "reassurance service" for elderly
- ❑ Participating in "Meals on Wheels" program
- ❑ Reading books to the sightless or ill
- ❑ Literacy volunteers
- ❑ 4-H program, city parks, gardens
- ❑ Big Brothers/Big Sisters
- ❑ Little League
- ❑ Sponsoring Girl or Boy Scout troop
- ❑ Volunteering in city library, historical sites
- ❑ Assisting in building/repairing community playgrounds
- ❑ School volunteers
- ❑ Cooperating in Friendly Visitors programs
- ❑ Peace Corps
- ❑ Red Cross

How about supporting agencies which support you, as a retired person?

❑ Does your community have a Council on Aging?

❑ Are there organized groups of retired people in your area?

Find out where retired people meet for concerted action and join others like yourself. Ideas will emerge as you discuss your problems and your concerns. *You can do something to help others and to help yourself*…if you do not insist on working *by yourself.*

Visit your Senior Center, if you have one in your community. If you do not have a Senior Center, discuss with other adults how you can organize one. It can be the center of meetings which will provide the satisfactions once afforded by your job. It can be the center from which community service ideas will originate. It can provide opportunity for participation that keeps you young, and for sharing that brings you joy.

VOLUNTEERING: WHEN TO BEGIN

You do not have to wait for retirement to begin volunteer work. If you are still working, now is the time to engage in voluntary service. You can start on a limited basis, as time permits, and extend your service in retirement. The important thing is to develop a way of channeling the extra time you will have in retirement.

In addition to making better use of your free time, there are other benefits to be derived from volunteer service. Such work often leads to new friendships, educational, cultural and social activities.

Your new friends and activities are especially important if you have not maintained outside interests during your working years. By starting volunteer work now, you will be going into retirement with an established circle of friends whose interests are similar to your own.

Another plus for volunteer service—it is good work experience. If you are thinking about starting a second career when you retire, volunteer work can gain for you the background needed to reach your goal. Or if you are considering a certain line of work but have some doubts, volunteer service may be just the way to help you know for sure.

BOOKS THAT CAN HELP

The Three Boxes of Life: And How to Get Out of Them. Richard N. Bolles. 1999. ISBN# 0-9-13-668-58-3. $18.95 plus $4.50 for handling. Order from: Ten Speed Press, P.O. Box 7123, Berkeley, CA 94707. www.tenspeed.com

FOR AN EXCITING RETIREMENT...

Perhaps it's time to think about school for yourself. Tens of thousands of others approaching 65, or who are already retired, are attending classes this fall. A large majority are attending school part-time.

Today's trend is to sign up for classes that will make life and retirement more exciting, and perhaps more profitable.

Of course, you don't have to go to college for a continuing education. Your purposes might be served as well if you take adult education courses available through your public school system or offered by one of the various organizations—perhaps your YMCA or YMHA—that sponsors courses.

If you have a lively mind and an interest in improving it, you almost certainly can find educational opportunities (often free or at a minimum charge) that can open up a world of vast horizons in your later years.

The sharpness of a mind generally is blunted, not by age but by disuse. This can happen at any age.

Those reasonably healthy can maintain skills

CHECK OUT YOUR:

Local Library
Nearest College
Community Center
Local YMCA/YMHA
Board of Education

and abilities well into, and perhaps beyond, their 80's. The ability to learn new things is also maintained. If mental responses are slowed a little, this is more than offset by the fact that the older you are, the greater your advantage in being able to apply to learning a background of knowledge and experience younger people have not acquired.

So—don't hold back. And don't feel that it's eccentric to go back to school, or shy away from being taught by a younger person.

Many are interested in making up for years when going to school was not possible. Continuing education courses offer opportunities to take elementary and high school level equivalency courses, leading to diplomas. In some programs it is possible to obtain credit for "life experiences"—your jobs and activities count toward a degree.

Explore the possibilities of the many courses available that are intended to enrich the lives of adults in your community, or to prepare them for better or different jobs during their working years—or in retirement.

There are many exciting cultural courses: Great Books classes, history studies, courses in art or music appreciation, current issues, politics, philosophy and similar subjects.

Some are practical. These often include income management and investing, health, home and auto repairs, legal and tax matters, sewing, cooking and the like. Courses like these can be invaluable during your retirement years, when money is tight. The skills you learn can not only give you personal satisfaction, but they can save you money—a real inflation fighter.

COURSES OF ALL KINDS

Other classes are hobby-oriented. Many continuing education programs include courses in such things as art, photography, crafts, golf, and other sports. Hobby-oriented courses offer chances to explore ways to spend your retirement leisure enjoyably.

Many are directed toward present or future jobs. Courses in bookkeeping, computer programming, office skills, real estate, medical technology, and the basics of starting your own business are available in most communities. Costs vary greatly, but usually there is a Senior Citizen discount.

If you are among those who didn't go to college or complete college work toward a degree, now is a good time to get started. Or if you are among those with keen interests in any field, it's a good time to satisfy them by looking through a college catalog and signing up for a course or two. The range of classes is wider than in adult education programs sponsored by public school systems or local organizations, and the subject matter probably more advanced.

Many colleges and universities run extension courses, also known as continuing education programs, in centers around the college area. Many are offered at night or during weekends. They may or may not be credit courses—that is, giving credits toward eventual college or university degrees. While the costs may be high, discounts are often given to those in their 60's or older.

To find out what is available and what the entrance requirements will be, you should contact the Dean of Admissions (or the Dean of Older Students, a relatively new post at some institutions) at your local college or university. Some schools have the same requirements for older applicants as for younger ones, but many do not require a high school diploma for older applicants whose backgrounds suggest an aptitude for college level work.

If you take courses for credit, you will have to meet the same requirements as younger students:

attending classes, doing assigned work, turning in papers, and taking tests and examinations. You also will be graded, but don't let that make you nervous—surveys show that older students do as well as those in other age groups.

COURSES TO FIT YOUR SCHEDULE

Those really interested in college may find "weekend college" programs in their area. Classes are scheduled on Saturdays and Sundays, usually lasting two or three hours instead of one to cover a whole week's work in a day. It's hard work but a good way to get a diploma.

All the above applies also to Junior and Community Colleges, which may be more convenient than four-year schools to many who are interested in continuing education. There are other points in their favor: local two-year colleges are often free to older applicants, and ordinarily *anyone* who is interested can sign up *without* questions about high school backgrounds.

You may have heard about correspondence courses, either part of college extension programs or offered privately. These can be a good idea for independent learning, though being in a class where questions are asked and comments are made, is beneficial to the learning process and your enjoyment.

Be particularly careful when you see private organizations offer courses in computer programming, art, writing, and other subjects—often with

IT'S SMART TO GO BACK TO SCHOOL... WHAT'S YOUR REASON?

LEARNING HOW TO REPAIR MY CAR!

JUST FOR PLEASURE!

START MY OWN BUSINESS!

KEEPING UP WITH CURRENT EVENTS!

COOKING CLASS!

COMPUTER TRAINING!

A BETTER JOB!

REASONS TO RETURN TO SCHOOL

To make new friends.	To comply with the suggestions of someone else.
To be accepted by others.	To help me earn a degree, diploma or certificate.
To satisfy an inquiring mind.	To have a few hours away from responsibilities.
To prepare for community service.	To get a break in the routine of home or work.
To learn just for the joy of learning.	To become acquainted with congenial people.
To seek knowledge for its own sake.	To supplement a narrow previous education.
To improve my ability to serve mankind.	To provide a contrast for the rest of my life.
To maintain or improve my social position.	To gain insight into my personal problems.
To stop myself from becoming a "vegetable."	To gain insight into human relations.
To provide a contrast to my previous education.	To improve my social relationships.
To help me earn a degree, diploma or certificate.	To learn just for the sake of learning.
To overcome the frustration of day-to-day living.	To become a more effective citizen.
To carry out the recommendation of some authority.	To escape an unhappy relationship.
To share a common interest with my spouse or friend.	To participate in group activity.
To improve my ability to participate in community work.	To get relief from boredom.
To fulfill a need for personal associations and friendships.	To keep up with others.
To acquire knowledge to help with other educational courses.	To escape television.

promises of "sure" employment or income. Check with a Better Business Bureau before you sign up.

Many who are interested primarily in "recreational" improvement of minds pay too little attention to local libraries, museums, galleries, and even television as aids to a continuing education. Local institutions often sponsor lecture series or talks on topics of the day. These are mini-educational programs that often can be interesting.

TV offers much more than entertainment programs. In many areas, courses in general education or university studies are worthwhile whether you sign up to receive course material and to have your work monitored, or whether you just audit the programs aired.

Now that you know more about what you can find in education, nothing should stop you from having a happier, more interesting retirement.

All it takes is a little time, a little energy, and some motivation to get you started on the way to being a younger-feeling, more alive, and more stimulated person.

RETIREMENT: EARLY OR LATER?

When should you retire? This is fast becoming the number one question on the minds of many American workers. Only a short time ago, the decision when to retire was probably not yours to make. But recent changes in the law and more flexible pension plans now give many workers exciting new retirement options.

This means that most American workers now have a broader choice to make when they try to pinpoint a retirement age. For many workers today, the time span is from 50 to 70—a 20 year time period. With greater freedom in selecting a date for retirement, it is important that you choose carefully. As we shall see, retiring before or after the right time may lead to problems. The right choice will help to insure a successful retirement.

YOUR OPTIONS

You no longer are required to retire at 70. The 1986 amendments to the Federal Age Discrimination in Employment Act bars mandatory retirement except under a few specific circumstances (under certain conditions, companies may enforce mandatory retirement practices for policy-making executives). Now, older workers must be assessed for continued employment solely on a basis of ability—not age. This means you have three options:

❑ You can retire voluntarily at 65, as before, and begin collecting Social Security.

❑ You can elect to continue working.

❑ You can take early retirement. The liberalization of pension plans in recent years has resulted in a rise in retirement before 65. Others who are not covered by a pension plan may continue to work as long as possible.

Current Social Security law gradually increases the retirement age from 65 to 67 by the year 2027. The chart below indicates the age at which you can retire and receive full benefits (see page 29 for a discussion of how your Social Security benefits will be affected by a decision to retire early).

AGE TO RECEIVE FULL SOCIAL SECURITY BENEFITS

Year of Birth	Full Retirement Age
1937 or earlier	65
1938	65 and 2 months
1939	65 and 4 months
1940	65 and 6 months
1941	65 and 8 months
1942	65 and 10 months
1943-1954	66
1955	66 and 2 months
1956	66 and 4 months
1957	66 and 6 months
1958	66 and 8 months
1959	66 and 10 months
1960 and later	67

WHEN TO RETIRE

Whether or not you elect to stay on the job past retirement age, the option you choose should depend on your personal circumstances. You may want to quit earlier, take your pension and find an easier job. You may want to work on past 65 to meet continuing high costs for medical care, the children's college costs or other needs. Or you may be ready to quit at 65 to take life easier.

Whatever you do, whenever you retire, remember that you face psychological changes. Idleness may give you a feeling of guilt and shame, a loss of self-esteem, a withdrawal from society.

It doesn't have to be that way. In retirement you must face yourself afresh. Keep free of self-pity and bitterness, accept your situation, compensate for whatever losses might come, and remind yourself that what is important is not *what you've lost,* but *what you still have and still can do.*

In short, learn to focus on retirement as a positive experience. Retirement is a new beginning; it gives you the chance to develop and expand your interests in ways that were not possible during your working years. Before retirement, much of your time is taken up by the day-to-day necessity of work. In retirement, the end of that routine means the beginning of new opportunities.

EARLY RETIREMENT

Today, only about 57% of men aged 55-64 are in the labor force, down from 83% in 1970 while 42% of women aged 55-64 are in the work force. The early-retirement trend partly reflects voluntary departures, before the traditional retirement age of 65. In recent years, however, huge numbers of employees have been pushed into premature retirement, the victims of corporate downsizings.

A major change in the retirement age is coming. The reason the next crop of retirees may stay working longer is primarily economics. They won't be as able to retire at 55, or maybe even at 65, because of inadequate savings, reduced employer benefits and the likely scaling-back of what the federal government will provide.

As the rules governing Social Security payments gradually change, with full benefits eventually not kicking in until age 67 instead of 65, that could be a further incentive to keep people working. Even without such a change in the rules, though, many retiring workers could be in for a shock at the size of their monthly checks.

It is probably true that today's older workers are better able to keep plugging away at a job. These 60-year-olds are healthier than those a generation ago. Moreover, fewer jobs now require heavy physical labor. Reeducating and retraining of older workers could prolong their work lives.

To those asking the question, should I retire early?, you should consider these questions:

Why? Retire early to what? Do you have a new life waiting for you?

For some workers, early retirement is not necessarily a free and happy choice. As many as one out of every five men who leave jobs before 65 do so because of their health or physical condition. A somewhat higher percentage of women retiring early cite such reasons.

If the work is getting too demanding, and particularly if doctors recommend taking things easier in your 50's or early 60's, retiring may be the right thing to do.

However, most are still physically fit and able to continue on the job up to 65—and beyond that common retirement age. Those who are should consider carefully the pros and cons of early retirement, the possible rewards and the potential pitfalls. Those who have worked for three or four decades will find inactivity difficult. They must substitute something for work.

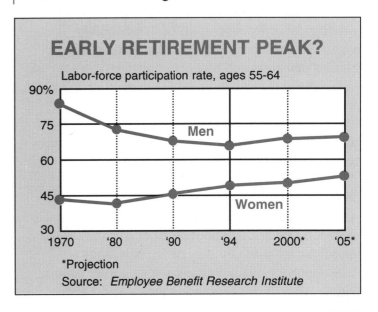

EARLY RETIREMENT PEAK?

Labor-force participation rate, ages 55-64

*Projection

Source: *Employee Benefit Research Institute*

They should have a carefully thought out new life ahead. While that is true for everyone who retires, regardless of their age, it is particularly true for those retiring early. Younger retirees must look ahead not for an average decade or two, as those 65 must, but as long as three decades.

If you're going to start a new life early, ask yourself what is it going to be like? Early retirement is not for everyone: you must be ready for it and able to take it in full stride and enjoy it: most of all, you must be able to afford it, not just at the time of early retirement but through the years to come.

CAN YOU AFFORD TO RETIRE?

You should be aware of the impact of inflation on those who retire. It is a problem now, and it is likely to continue to be one. While the rate of inflation has fortunately been considerably reduced, it is still a factor; a four percent annual rate of inflation amounts to over a 20% rise in the cost of living in just five years.

Remember, dollars are worth less, year to year. It's hard to live with inflation while you're working. It will be even harder when you retire on a fixed income. Costs go up and, except for cost-of-living changes in Social Security benefits, income of retirees may not keep up with living costs.

Retirement on a full pension and with full Social Security benefits is difficult in years of inflation. The problems will be considerably worse for those who elect to retire earlier with smaller pensions and Social Security payments.

Unless you can retire early and build up your reserves through a new job, a new business or a new career, you will probably be better off economically to work longer and concentrate on accumulating reserves for a more secure future.

However, dollars are not the only thing to think about.

Work satisfaction is another important factor in making decisions about whether to continue on the job as long as you can, or to retire early.

Sometimes it is better to have a simpler future, with less income, and not as much socked away, than to spend additional years in a job that you dread going to.

It is hard to put a price on happiness, but it sometimes must be done.

RETIRE TO A SECOND CAREER

Do you have a job waiting for you? Remember, if you are considering early retirement, it's easy to talk casually about "resting up" for a while and then getting a new job.

But those who do not have highly marketable skills could run into a difficult time in a period of high unemployment.

If you are in your 50's and do not have a job waiting for you, be wary of retiring early unless you have sufficient reserves to make additional income unnecessary: you might find it's awfully hard to find the new job you now take for granted.

If you are considering early retirement without plans to take another job, full- or part-time. What then?

Are you really ready for all the leisure you'll have? Can you fill your time with community service, educational opportunities, hobbies, travel, sports, cards—whatever?

It sounds easy to do, but it isn't for many retirees.

Remember how many years you will have ahead if you retire early, and make sure, by advance planning, that you can make them active and fulfilling years.

Retire early if you can enjoy your later years free of financial worries and free of boredom.

Stay on the job if you aren't sure you can. (See Chapter 9)

MAKING THE DECISION

Every man or woman approaching retirement must make the decision to retire at 65 (or earlier) or go past 65 on a basis of individual circumstances.

The first, and perhaps biggest question is: Do you need to continue working?

For example, are you paying off a mortgage and need to continue receiving a regular paycheck to do it comfortably? Do you still have a child or children in college and need your regular wages or salary to meet steadily climbing costs?

Do you have some other important financial need that can best be met by continuing on your regular job beyond 65? Under such circumstances, the right to work on can be a blessing.

If regular work is such a habit for you that the very thought of breaking it by retiring is a psychological problem, then perhaps working beyond 65 is your answer.

But remember, in the long run the substitution of new things—work and play and just plain relaxing—may be better for you.

On the other hand, consider this: the longer you go on, the harder it will be to retire—and someday you will have to. It is easier to change a lifestyle at an active 65 than at 70.

You will adapt more easily to the things you would enjoy doing but haven't had an opportunity to do, and it will be easier to slip into a new, less arduous job if you want to supplement your retirement pay.

Before you decide, try doing the following: with the help of your employee benefits office at work or someone in the nearest Social Security office, find out whether staying on the job beyond age 65 would substantially increase your eventual retirement benefits.

For some, particularly those who have been jobless over long periods and have changed jobs frequently so that years of service for one employer haven't accumulated sufficiently, working beyond 65 could be a step toward a more adequate income in retirement.

RETIREMENT CHECKLIST

If you are considering early retirement, try answering these questions:

❑ Do you have something definite you want to do after early retirement? Is there something you have always wanted to do that you can undertake in your late 50's or early 60's? A second, deeply satisfying career, perhaps?

❑ Can you earn enough or have you saved enough to bridge the financial gap between what you will get as a pension if you retire early and the full amount that you'd get at 65?

❑ Have you factored in inflation? Keep in mind that if inflation holds steady at 3%, $1,000 of today's dollars will be worth less than $554 in 2020. People age 60 today have a life expectancy of 24 more years.

❑ Have you planned sufficiently for early retirement? With your spouse and other members of your family? Planning for retirement at 65 should begin five to ten years before that.

❑ Financially, are major obligations (mortgages, children's education, installment credit and the like) paid off or under control?

❑ Have you thought about medical and hospital insurance between the time you leave your job and group plans and when you will become eligible for Medicare?

❑ Are you sure that early retirement will make you and your spouse—and all of your family—happier? That you really want it?

CHECK BENEFITS & PLAN

If you're thinking about retiring early, check with your Social Security office to find out how much you'll forfeit in benefits, and with your company personnel office to find out how your pension will be affected. Retiring at 62 could cost about 20% of the benefits you'd be due if you worked to age 65.

Before you retire, start checking on the documents you will need to claim Social Security benefits: Social Security card and that of your spouse. Proofs of ages of both of you, preferably birth certificates. Your marriage license. Get them together and in order.

Decide on pension options, medical insurance needs and options for handling mortgage or other financial obligations that will continue after retirement.

Decide, also, on whether automobiles and appliances should be replaced while your income is at maximum; it's generally a good idea to replace appliances over ten years old. And consider your basic clothing needs.

Above all, begin developing retirement interests and activities. If married, these should be both individual and joint.

JUST BEFORE YOU RETIRE...

When your retirement time is approaching, here are some things you should do:

❑ Have a medical checkup while you are still covered by your company's medical program; it will save you money.

❑ Register with your Social Security office about three months *in advance* of your retirement. It takes that long to process applications. Your spouse should go with you. Take the documents you need, including a copy of your last two W-2 tax forms, the withholding statement, and your spouse's tax papers if both of you are working. (See page 34)

❑ Check with former employers to find out whether you might be due partial pensions based on their contributions to pension plans in your behalf when you were employed. Vesting plans vary. Many who retire lose money because they neglect to check with former employers. (See Chapter 2)

❑ Retirement benefits are available under some conditions to war veterans with limited incomes, or to widows of veterans. To qualify, veterans must be permanently or totally disabled due either to a service or non-service injury. If you think you might qualify, check with your nearest Veterans' Administration office.

❑ Most important, make realistic plans for day-to-day living in retirement. You should have estimates of what your financial needs will be for living costs, housing, insurance, health care, transportation, utilities, clothing, recreation and miscellaneous costs. With retirement day approaching, review them carefully; in inflationary times, living cost estimates made earlier may no longer be accurate. In addition to estimates of what you'll need, reassess what you'll have.

- Sit down with a personnel officer of your company to work out exactly what your pension will be—and the options open to you in monthly benefits. If you elect to collect monthly checks payable only until you die, your income will be larger but a surviving spouse will be left without pension checks. Your spouse will have to agree in writing to this arrangement. It's the law. An alternative is to take a lesser amount that will continue after the death of the retiree. There are a number of joint-life plans based on actuarial tables for life expectancy of the employee and his or her spouse. You should know your options.

- Check with your company on how and when pension checks will come to you; what options are open to you on accrued vacation or sick leave time (often you can get a lump-sum payment); whether life insurance carries over or must be switched from a group plan to an individual policy and what could be done about continuing health and hospitalization insurance.

- If you are retiring, but plan to continue to work in a second career, get in advance, a copy of the pamphlet "You Can Work and Still Get Social Security" available from your Social Security office.

In a nutshell, when you retire, be ready. Know what retirement will mean and how you will accommodate to it.

WHEN YOU RETIRE

So you've retired. What then?

Your advance planning should have given you an answer to that question. However, here are things you should consider:

- If you have received a lump-sum payment from a qualified pension or profit-sharing plan, talk to someone at your bank or in a conservative brokerage or financial house about how it best can be used to meet your future needs. Don't consider the big check a windfall, and go on a spending spree. Remember, it's taxable money. **You may**

avoid an immediate tax when you have higher income by having your employer transfer the money directly to an Individual Retirement Account (IRA) within 60 days. (See page 16)

- If you enrolled in Social Security three months before retirement, your first check should arrive in the month after you retire. (see chart on page 34)

- Depending upon restrictions in your pension plan, many retirees are able to continue full- or part-time employment. Check with your personnel or State employment office.

- Medicare provides hospital coverage after an annual deductible and a certain percentage of medical expenses after another deductible. Chapter 7 provides details of the provisions of both Hospital and Medical coverage by Medicare. These are subject to change by Congressional action. There are supplemental insurance policies you may buy. Check their benefits carefully before you buy.

- Your tax position changes with retirement. Social Security benefits are taxable if your adjusted gross income plus non-taxable interest and half of your Social Security benefit is more than a base amount (the base

for an individual is $25,000—for a couple filing jointly it is $32,000), but part or all of your pension will be subject to income taxes. So will income you may have from part-time or other work, and from most other sources. Unless you take another regular job, you won't have money withheld to cover continuing taxes. Be prepared to handle more tax work —and tax payments—on your own. If you have any questions, call the nearest Internal Revenue Service office for answers.

❑ If you have your savings for retirement in growth and tax-deferred investments, check with your banker or broker about the advisability of changes to income and security accounts. (See Financial Planning, Chapter 2)

❑ Consider ways to cut costs. Does your auto insurer offer a premium rate to drivers of retirement age who do *not* use cars to drive to work? Some do. If your car is more than four years old, check with your agent about dropping the collision insurance in your policy; it might not be worth the cost. And if you plan to buy a new car, check on insurance rates for the cars you're interested in: rates differ from model to model.

❑ Reassess the adequacy of your home insurance every year. With inflation, repair and replacement costs are rising year to year. Be sure you are sufficiently protected against losses from fire or other hazards. Check with your life insurance agent as to whether you can convert your present coverage to a paid-up policy and save on further premiums. You may not need the policy.

❑ If you want to work, there are agencies in most counties or cities that help older workers find part-time or full-time employment. Any local agency that works with older people can refer you to one. You may also register with an employment agency that furnishes temporary help if you have a marketable job experience. (See Chapter 9)

❑ If you don't want a job but want to keep busy, investigate local volunteer service opportunities. Volunteers are in short supply everywhere.

❑ Don't try to adapt yourself overnight to your new life and your changed circumstances.

Go at it slowly and carefully, remembering that retirement is not an end but a beginning.

❑ Check into recreation, education, civic activities—even politics—and community service that offer enough in the way of a new opportunity to provide a sound basis for a new life in retirement.

FACTS TO CONSIDER

The years you'll spend in retirement. They can be easily 15 to 25 years. Americans are living longer.

Inflation will reduce the value of your retirement dollars.

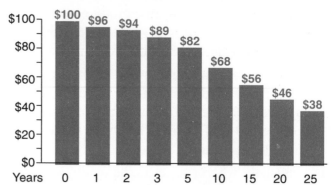

THE BUYING POWER OF $100 OVER TIME

Each year the buying power of $100 decreases as the price of goods increases with inflation. This chart assumes a 4% average inflation rate. Social Security is indexed for inflation, your pension may not be, and your investments should earn 4% after taxes to stay even.

Social Security is indexed for inflation. But the index doesn't fully cover the increased costs of medical care.

Your pension may be indexed, many are not. If your employer shifts your pension to a "Cash Balance Plan" you maybe adversely affected.

Your investment should earn the rate of inflation plus taxes to stay even.

Health care costs continue to escalate Medicare does not cover a number of health items that you'll have to pay yourself (see page 66).

WOMEN LIVE LONGER

Women live longer than men. That's a simple biological fact that should be kept in mind in retirement planning.

Generally, it isn't. It's something we don't like to think about or sit down and talk about. Still, we must face the fact that an estimated 85% of all married women in the United States will be widowed.

Six out of ten women in the pre-retirement age group, 55 to 64, are married, four out of ten are either widowed, divorced or have never married. For the age group 65 to 74, somewhat fewer are still married. Both groups, in planning for their retirement, face similar concerns and some that are different. For both, understanding one's financial situation is of fundamental importance.

Women who never married, or have been

	LIFE EXPECTANCY			
	——Male——		——Female——	
Age	Expectancy	Years	Expectancy	Years
50	75.5	25.5	79.6	29.6
55	76.7	21.7	80.5	25.5
60	78.2	18.2	81.7	21.7
65	80.0	15.0	83.2	18.2
70	82.1	12.1	85.0	15.0
75	84.6	9.6	87.1	12.1

widowed or divorced, have had some experience in handling their financial affairs, while some married women left these details to their husbands. There are, of course, many who are as able as their husbands to list family assets, debts and otherwise summarize and grasp their financial position.

MOM'S WORKING—DAD'S NOT

In today's work environment, with company downsizing and early retirement, the expectations of many families have been affected. Many men find themselves in retirement much earlier than anticipated. Meanwhile, their wives continue to work. This creates a new dynamic in the home and in the husband-wife relationship that can be difficult for both to adjust to.

Many successfully make the transition. Those that do, approach their unexpected new circumstances as an opportunity—even if not welcomed—to start a new career or pursue long put-off objectives. There is a greater need for planning, though, both financial and otherwise. The many chapters in this book can help.

ASK YOURSELF QUESTIONS

Women's longevity makes it necessary for them to face difficult questions:

❑ How many years can I expect to live with my spouse after retirement?
❑ How many years will one of us be likely to live alone?
❑ Whether married or single, what is my life expectancy?

By now you've bought insurance, made your will, may have even discussed retirement with spouse, friend, family. Have you, however, been realistic and honest?

With age, married or not, comes death of loved ones.

Along with the marriage partner and probable family, we develop a sense of interdependence. We share decisions and responsibilities and our identity is strongly and inevitably intertwined with our partner. Our marriage and family life offers a source of love, security, emotional support, and companionship.

What happens when a person who has spent adult life in partnership with another is faced with the reality of being alone. The prospect of becoming widowed, of ending your shared experience with your marriage partner, is almost beyond thought. Still, you would be far better off by giving serious thought to how you can be somewhat prepared for that eventuality.

The purpose of this section is to provide a guide for that thinking. You can plan and prepare many of your affairs with your partner as you always have, and do it more securely and easily than if you were alone and under stress and emotional upheaval.

Being prepared is not an indication that you are preparing for the imminent death of your partner. The chances are that you have many happy years together ahead of you. But if an accidental death or fatal illness should occur, at least you will be in a position to carry on with and manage your life.

WIDOWHOOD: BEING PREPARED

"How can anyone be prepared for widowhood?"
It may not be possible to be ready for the wrenching shock of learning that your spouse is dying or has died. One thing you can do in this regard is to understand something of the emotions you are feeling and realize that it is good to grieve. Grief is the way our minds become reconciled to losing a loved one.

And we may feel other things besides grief. We may feel guilt—guilty for not having done certain things when our spouse was alive. We may feel angry—angry at being abandoned and left alone, at having to be without the awareness of where certain things are, or what needs to be done. We may feel lost—the old routines and patterns of living are gone. There is no one to eat breakfast with in the morning, and no one to talk to at night. We are at a loss about what to do or where to go. We may feel despair—despair so deep that we want to die. There will also be many painful days, when holidays come, or anniversaries, or birthdays. We think back to what was and now is no longer, and we feel terribly down.

AFTERWARD

The months following the death of someone we love are difficult and critical times in life. They are difficult, because we have to deal with all kinds of emotions, without the help of someone with whom we used to share many of our worries and cares. They are critical times because we are starting out, on our own, to make a new life for ourselves. We will have to learn new skills, do

things we never dreamed of doing, make friends and find new ways to spend our time usefully.

No one can prevent this time in our life from being painful. People can help and will help, if we let them.

We may need the help of an attorney or a financial counselor for legal and monetary matters. There will be many matters to take care of involving taxes, property, inheritance, Social Security, insurance and the like. It will cost us some money to get help with such things, but it may cost us more not to. Very soon, after the funeral, we will want to take care of these matters: 1) processing the will, 2) freeing bank accounts, 3) changing title on property, car, stock, etc., 4) settling unpaid bills, while keeping accurate and complete records, 5) applying for Social Security funeral benefits, and 6) filing life insurance claims.

Other affairs that we must take care of, but that we need not be concerned with for awhile, are income taxes, budgeting, seeing that our own will is as we want it, inheritance and estate taxes, and possibly others if there are minor children or dependents. Keep in close communication with a knowledgeable friend, or attorney, to be sure all necessary tasks are accomplished.

During the period after the death of our spouse we may also need the emotional support that counseling, by a psychologist or minister, can give, particularly if we find that our grieving does not lessen after about six weeks. But most of all we need to help ourselves. We need to find the power within ourselves to start a new life and to begin to discover who we are, what our potentials are, and what possibilities lie before us.

THINGS TO DO

Planning for both married and single should begin in the mid-50's or earlier. Don't be discouraged if you are well past that point.

Assess your assets and debits as soon as possible. Summarize your whole family financial position. This is difficult for women who customarily left the handling of these matters of business entirely to a husband.

EXPAND YOUR INTERESTS AND MAKE NEW FRIENDS

Take a class—at your local community college or adult educational center.

Join a club—clubs are organized for almost any interest.

Attend church or synagogue—and participate in its activities—you'll never be lonesome.

Volunteer—the first person you help is yourself.

Politics—make a contribution to our political life and work with active people interested in public issues.

Travel—check with Elderhostel 877-426-8056 or www.elderhostel.org or Interhostel (University of New Hampshire, 6 Garrison Ave., Durham, NH 03824-3529 or www.learn.unh.edu) for group travel worldwide sponsored by American colleges. Once you participate in a session, you'll be back year after year. Send for their catalogs.

Join your local museum—and participate in its activities. They need volunteers.

Be active in your alumni group—see old friends and make new ones.

Your local school—it could use your services.

For all women, *now* is the time to understand your financial status. Don't wait for retirement. If you set your mind to it and seek advice you'll find it far less bewildering than you might have thought. It's just a matter of attention and faith in yourself.

Looking ahead to retirement: even if it's a decade or more away, husbands and wives should work together to prepare and maintain a careful inventory of what the family has—of all assets—and what they owe. They should consider together all insurance policies (life, health and hospitalization, accident, household, auto or whatever) and list them, noting the names of companies, numbers of the policies,

REVIEW FINANCIAL MATTERS

- ❑ Do both you and your spouse review together your family's financial obligations and resources?
- ❑ Are both you and your spouse aware of where your money is kept (bank, investments, property, etc.) and the status of major policies such as insurance?
- ❑ Are complete financial records, including names of your lawyer, insurance agent, bank, and broker, filed in an organized manner that husband, wife or relative can refer to?
- ❑ Are children involved in money matters that affect them? Are they, or someone you trust, in a position to help manage your family's finances should the need arise?

names of agents and where the policies are kept. And they should make and update as necessary, legal wills, one for each partner, and note where they can be found.

Too many husbands think they do wives a favor by assuming responsibilities for handling bank accounts, bill payments, debts, investments and other money matters; they seem to think of this as a husband's job. Instead of a favor, those who exclude wives from financial affairs may be creating a major problem for spouses who might suddenly be confronted with a need to cope responsibly with such matters.

The result could be headaches and heartaches for a spouse in a time of crisis—and possibly extra financial costs.

Women must have the knowledge of family affairs and experience in handling day-to-day financial matters if—in an emergency—they are to handle the chores alone. Shared handling of financial matters will make lone decisions easier.

Working together, each of you will have a good idea of how the family stands financially. While this will not ease the grief, it can reduce confusion and unnecessary strain at a very trying time.

WILL YOUR WIFE BE SECURE?

That's another question you have to think about together. Is the husband's life insurance adequate? If he is retired, would his pension terminate with his death? If he is still working, would his pension program provide for his widow if he dies before retirement? What help would Social Security be, either way? How about health insurance?

KNOW YOUR PENSION, INSURANCE

Many working men—and women—do not know enough about their pension plans. They know, only vaguely, what they can expect in monthly payments after retirement at age 65. They have not read, or have forgotten, the fine print in pension material furnished by employers.

It is a good idea to take a close look at pension plans to find answers to the questions we asked. **Check the listed beneficiary of IRA's, 401 (k)'s, stock investment plan, insurance and other savings plans that either spouse may have. Make sure you keep copies of your beneficiary forms in a safe place along with your other estate documents.**

You should check on what would happen to your widow's health and hospital insurance coverage, particularly under group insurance programs. If there are any provisions for extending coverage, explore the possibilities.

About life insurance: It's a good idea to review the amount of coverage you have in light of the rising cost of living. What might have been adequate coverage when policies were taken out, might be inadequate now.

DECISIONS WIDOWS MUST MAKE

Many women find that after the death of a husband, they face, in addition to loneliness and grief, worries about budgeting and managing money, along with a lot of other problems that were the husband's responsibility.

For some, the necessity of tackling such new tasks is therapeutic. For others, it is added strain and more unhappiness.

One of the first and toughest decisions a widow must make is what to do with the money from insurance policies and from her husband's estate. She may suddenly have what seems to be a great deal of capital.

If she is inexperienced in handling capital, she could feel overwhelmed. It is a good idea for a husband and wife to plan well in advance what can be done. Sound guidance is important—at any time.

In regard to family savings and investment programs, be wary, set clear objectives based on projected annual budget needs, get expert counseling, but avoid letting capital stay idle and unproductive because of uncertainties about what should be done and what should not.

Annuities can provide an assured income for life, but they limit flexibility. Once funds are committed, they cannot be retrieved or shifted.

Flexibility is necessary because of inflation, and because needs vary. It's a good idea to explore the variety of investment possibilities early, in connection with pre-retirement planning, and establish a sound program that provides a basis for the use of insurance and other money by the widow.

SOCIAL SECURITY AND WOMEN

Changes made in the Social Security law in 1983 added additional benefits for women. Benefits will be continued for surviving divorced spouses and disabled widows and widowers who remarry.

An eligible divorced spouse, age 62 or over, whose divorce has been in effect at least two years can

---

Social Security: What Every Woman Absolutely Needs to Know

For a free copy write to: AARP, Fulfillment, 601 E Street, NW, Washington, DC 20049. Ask for Publication No. D14117.

---

become eligible for benefits, based on the earnings of a former spouse who is eligible for retirement, regardless of whether the former spouse has retired or applied for benefits. Check with Social Security on benefits you expect to receive. See Chapter 3.

DO NOT SIGN A PENSION WAIVER...

Do not sign a pension waiver until you understand your choices. The 1984 Retirement Equity Act makes it easier for women to receive retirement benefits in defined benefit pension plans, either their husband's or their own. A defined benefit pension plan is based on both your years of service and wages.

The Act requires that in a *Defined Benefit Plan* a spouse must give written permission before an employee could choose a plan that would stop payments upon the employee's death instead of continuing payments to the surviving spouse.

The Act requires the payment of a pension to the spouse of a worker who was fully vested in a defined benefit plan or had become eligible for the plan after working a certain number of years, if the worker dies before reaching retirement age. The surviving spouse would receive the pension benefits at the earliest retirement age under his plan.

The Act lowers the age from 25 to 21 at which workers must be allowed to participate in a pension plan. The Act requires the pension plan to count the years of an employee's service from the time the person turns 18 in calculating when the employee had worked long enough to be eligible for a pension at retirement. The Act bars pension plans from counting a year maternity or paternity leave as a break in service.

Employees who have worked fewer than five years are permitted to take five years off without losing pension credit for earlier service.

The Act authorizes a Court to award a person part of their former spouse's pension as part of a divorce settlement.

IMPORTANT: The requirement of spousal consent does not apply in most instances to other savings, investments and retirement accounts such as IRA's, 401 (k)'s, insurance and stock participation plans. **Once again, it is very important to check.**

SURVIVOR BENEFITS

Before retiring, you will be asked whether you want to receive your defined benefit pension in a joint and survivor annuity, a lifetime benefit or a single lump sum payment. If the retiring spouse opts for the lifetime benefit or the single payment, both eliminate the widow/er's benefit. The retiree must have the spouse's consent and have them sign a spousal-consent form.

The form will list a series of options for you and your spouse to consider. The so called lifetime benefit usually provides the highest monthly benefit, so people are often tempted to select it. But it will pay only while the retired spouse is alive. It will end upon their death.

The joint and survivor annuity offers a smaller monthly payment. It guarantees a steady stream of income for two lifetimes, for the retiree and spouse. For women who expect to depend on their husband's pension as a source of income in retirement, this is generally the better option. For example, under a lifetime benefit while your husband is alive, the pension might be $1,600 a month. While under a joint and survivor annuity, with a 50% survivor benefit option, the benefit might be $1,300 a month. When your husband dies your survivor benefit would be $650 a month. Without the 50% option you would receive zero.

Do not assume that your husband understands his choices or the spousal consent form. He also may not realize that statistically you are likely to outlive him.

The last chance to make sure you receive a survivors pension is at the time of retirement. Don't sign away your rights unless you understand what you are giving up.

If your spouse worked for a federal, state or local government that does not require the payment of Social Security taxes, make sure he selects a joint and survivor annuity option for his pension, guaranteeing you a survivor's benefit. Unless you have your own Social Security and pension benefits, the spousal benefit is all you would be entitled to with the possible exception of supplemental security income (SSI).

WOMEN IN RETIREMENT: A CHECKLIST

- ❑ First and foremost, I do not sign anything I fail to understand. I refuse to be intimidated and will sign only when proper explanations have been given.
- ❑ I will plan ahead, recognizing that (1) it is never too late and that (2) it is never too early!
- ❑ I am on top of financial matters: I know where important documents are kept—pension, insurance, Social Security, etc.—as well as the names and addresses of our family's attorney, banker, broker, etc.
- ❑ My will is up-to-date, and I know where the original and copies are kept.
- ❑ I have reviewed health/hospital insurance coverage.
- ❑ If single, I have informed my attorney, banker, trusted friend or family member where my important documents are located, including my will.

- ❑ I am taking steps to enable me to handle a budget and finances that may (or already have) become my sole responsibility.
- ❑ I have looked into my own Social Security benefits and investigated recent additional ones for women.
- ❑ I understand my pension benefits.
- ❑ I pay attention to my diet—what and how much I eat and drink.
- ❑ I engage in some form of exercise a minimum of one hour, four times a week.
- ❑ I have a new interest: I've enrolled in a class, joined a group, traveled with Elderhostel….
- ❑ I agree that "age is a triumph not a burden" and that "in our old age we are free to be innovative, burst out and be creative."
- ❑ I am prepared to face retirement with enthusiasm, faith and optimism.

"THE DELIGHT I FEEL..."

"The delight I feel when any one of them wraps his or her arms around me, gives me a BIG hug, and says, "Hi, grandpa!"...it's priceless."
—A Los Angeles grandparent

DID YOU KNOW...?

- ❑ On the first Sunday after Labor Day each year, Americans around the country celebrate National Grandparents' Day.
- ❑ In the United States alone there are now at least 60 million grandparents.
- ❑ Nearly 5 million U.S. children live in extended families that include one or more grandparents in their household.
- ❑ 6.4% of grandparents are under the age of 45; 37.8% are 65 or older.

As the numbers above suggest, close to one in four Americans are grandparents. There was also a time in your life when *you* were a grandchild, hoping for a moment of your grandparents' time.

So what does this mean for you today? Obviously, it will affect you most if you are now a grandparent, for this is one "job" from which you will never retire.

Grandparenting is both a joy and a responsibility, linking your working days with your retired ones. It provides a sense of continuity and stability throughout the years, both for you and your grandchild. It is a way for you to keep feeling vital and important, and to make a contribution that is meaningful for all concerned. It is "a relatively pure form of love and affection" providing you with companionship, pleasure and pride.

When the lives of parents are fragmented by conflicting work schedules and marital discord, the children's spiritual development may be is overlooked. Should this occur, the love and guidance of grandparents can be so important. Grandparents can involve their grandchildren in their church or synagogue services. These efforts strengthen the moral fabric of families and, ultimately, society.

WORDS OF WISDOM

"Grandparenting is an art. Its principles can be stated in generalized words, but the practice has to be learned in the doing. The circumstances of each family are different, and the family members are unique personalities."

—Bill Bookman,
syndicated columnist

"Perhaps grandparents' most important function is as a reserve, to be there in case of need. Grandparents are the family National Guard, on stand-by duty to be called out in emergencies.... It's a positive thing that there are no strict rules on how a grandparent should behave. It gives them a lot of flexibility. They can serve a variety of functions precisely because it is so ambiguous."

—Gunhild Hagestad,
Northwestern University sociologist

WHAT TO DO WITH YOUR GRANDCHILDREN

❑ Contact your grandchild as often as possible. Visit if you live nearby or are able to travel. Make a phone call or send a postcard or videotape of yourself if you live far away.

❑ Accept your grandchildren as they are. Don't try to mold them to your own vision of the perfect grandchild.

❑ Encourage and answer questions. Treat them as important people and respect their thoughts and opinions.

❑ Take risks. The doorway to loving time with your grandchildren is blocked only by apprehension.

❑ Be your grandchildren's playmate and friend. Set aside your crossword puzzle or book and do what they want to do. Let them set the agenda.

❑ Take your grandchildren to the zoo, a museum, the ball game, or the movies. They'll remember the shared experience for a long time to come.

❑ Provide a link with the past; show your grandchild pictures of you as a child.

❑ Create memories and traditions. Tell your grandchild about your family history and traditions or your own childhood. Consider creating an oral or written history to hand down to your descendants.

❑ Show your grandchild that getting older is a happy time of life.

❑ Share triumphs as well as misfortunes.

❑ Prepare a cookbook with favorite family recipes

❑ Give your grandchild undivided attention by reading to them. For older children, increase their interest in reading by sharing books for future discussions.

TO BE A GRANDPARENT...

"There is much grandparents can do to enrich their grandchildren's experience.... Grandparents should be good listeners.... communication is nine-tenths of a good relationship.... They also play an important role in heightening the children's sense of security.... They are symbols of longevity and the extent of the human lifespan"

—Bill Bookman, syndicated columnist

THE SPICE IN YOUR LIFE

You will certainly be making a contribution to your grandchildrens' lives. In fact, a recent study found that grandparents are second only to parents in the influence they have on childrens' lives. In doing so, you will also be adding to your own sense of purpose and self-worth. It feels good to be a good grandparent, just as it feels good to be a good worker, community leader or parent.

Your grandkids can add spice to your life, just as you can to theirs. And you can pass on family traditions and history to them in the process.

With the increase in single-parent and two-income families, you may even find yourself playing an important or stabilizing role in the upbringing of your children's children.

Grandparents can be a big help by watching their grandchildren during those couple of hours each day after they're back from school, before their parents have arrived home from work.

STAYING IN TOUCH

You can make a great difference in your grandchild's life just by making a simple phone call, or sending a picture postcard. Send postcards to your grandchildren even before they can read, because the parents read the cards to them. Children love to receive postcards addressed just to them.

Another idea is to call up and speak to the grandchild, and when the grandchild says, "Do you want to speak to my mother?" say "No, I just called to speak to you."

Increase your grandparenting power by joining your grandchildren in a world where they enjoy spending a good amount of time. Learn about computers and join them online. Keep in touch with your loved ones by e-mail, help your grandchild with homework, write a grandparent's newsletter and benefit by the many web sites available on the internet.

LONG-DISTANCE GRANDPARENTING

You may be concerned that you live too far away from your grandchildren to be an active grandparent. With modern communication and transportation, the miles can be easily bridged. After all, your efforts—as simple as sending a birthday card, calling to ask about your grandchild's schoolwork or activities, or telling the child a story about your own life—will form lasting memories for your grandchildren.

One of the most important things a grandparent can do for a grandchild is simply to "be there".

Remember, a grandparent usually has a different role than that of a parent. Most grandchildren view their grandparents as a refuge from the daily demands of a disciplined home. Grandma and Grandpa can give kids something their parents may not be able to give—enough time. This is one of the things they need most.

This type of positive grandparent-grandchild relationship can be fostered with just a little extra effort on your part, whether you are one or one thousand miles away. A few minutes spent on the phone now will pay off handsomely later in the well-being of your grandchildren. And this, in turn, will make *you* feel better.

There is yet another possibility for grandparents who want to spend concentrated quality time with their grandchildren. You can invite your grandchild on a holiday or camp stay. Family reunions, combined with day vacation plans, offer retired grandparents a chance to select a suitable site and coordinate both transportation and various family schedules. These projects can yield rewards beyond what is required to make them happen.

CARING FOR GRANDKIDS

Perhaps your concern is not that you don't see your grandchildren enough, but rather that you see them more than you had originally bargained for. With your grandchildren's parents both working, you may have the responsibility of supervising the children's activities during the work day. You might even live with your grandchildren or be their primary caregivers. This is not an uncommon circumstance in the 1990's, and can be trying at times. If you find yourself in such a situation, it can only help to look at the bright side.

You are not alone. An estimated 4.7 million children live with one or both of their grandparents in some capacity, and 1.1 million of these children are actually being raised by grandparents rather than parents. Whether this is a result of choice or obligation, you should know that there are plenty of others just like you, and that support networks exist to assist you with legal, financial, and child-care concerns.

If both natural parents of your grandchild are either deceased or disabled, and your grandchild is dependent on you, the grandchild might qualify on your Social Security record. If the natural parents are not deceased or disabled, you might want to consider adopting the grandchild. When you do so, the child could qualify for Social Security benefits as your adopted child.

The value of your commitment to your grandchildren should not be underestimated. It may be hard work, but it's worth it. If you need help or support, contact the **Grandparent Information Center** (see box on page 116) or other organizations who understand your concerns. Your efforts will live on in the lives and minds of your grandchildren!

Remember, also, to take care of yourself. Your health and well-being are critical to the health and well-being of your grandchildren. While the opportunity to raise a grandchild may offer a "second chance" at parenting for some, the

and the unexpected demands of raising ...child may also result in stress-related ...sses such as high blood pressure and depression. ...or online support contact **Grands R Us** at www.grandsplace.com.

KEEPING YOUR SANITY

Here are some ideas grandparents have shared:

❑ Take some time for yourself and enjoy it. Take a bubble bath, read a book, talk to a friend.

❑ Pray - read the bible

❑ Hire a babysitter so you can go out and enjoy yourself or do errands alone. You can trade babysitting services with someone else, or offer to do something for someone in exchange for some babysitting time.

❑ Talk to people- let it out!

❑ Listen to the advice others give you. You may decide not to use it, but maybe some of it will be helpful.

❑ Ask for help, tell people what you need and what you would like them to do for you. If people ask what they can do for you, tell them!

❑ Give yourself a "Time Out". It gives you time to think and to cool off.

❑ Be open to your own feelings. You've got a

hard job to do. It can be frustrating and difficult. Know your limits and look for solutions that suit both your grandchild and you.

GRANDCHILDREN'S EDUCATION

Make time in your day for your grandchild's education. You can help your grandchild succeed in school if you:

❑ Set a regular homework time, before play time.

❑ Ask your grandchild's school about after-school tutoring.

❑ Read with your grandchildren every night at bedtime.

❑ Make regular fun outings to the library.

❑ Visit your grandchild's classroom, the guidance counselor, social worker, school psychologist and the principal. Ask how your grandchild is doing and what you can do to help. Let them know how you think they're doing.

❑ Get involved. Volunteer in your grandchild's classroom or offer to help out from home.

❑ If you drop off or pick up your grandchild at school, "drop in" on the classroom, say hello to the teacher and find out what your grandchild did that day.

❑ Make yourself known. Let the people in the

TIME SPENT WITH YOUR GRANDCHILDREN... ...WILL PLEASE YOUR GRANDCHILDREN... ...AND **YOU** TOO!

school know that you're interested in your grandchild's education.

❑ Keep in touch with your grandchild's teachers. Let them know that you care and that you're watching what's going on.

❑ Ask for face-to-face conferences with teachers, social workers, school psychologists, guidance counselors and principals.

❑ Ask what you can do at home to help your grandchild succeed in school. How can you reinforce at home what has been taught at school?

❑ Find out about your grandchild's homework and how to help with it.

❑ Don't forget to compliment your grandchildren when they do something good: bring home a good report card or help around the house. Consistent praise and "thank you's" are important.

DISCIPLINING GRANDCHILDREN

❑ "Making the Rules". Some call this setting limits or boundaries.

❑ Be clear about what types of behavior are OK and what types are not OK.

❑ Be sure the rules are appropriate for your grandchild's age and level of understanding.

❑ *Explain* the rules to your grandchild.

❑ *Discuss* the rules to make sure your grandchild understands them and make sure you agree on any specifics.

❑ Enforce the rules you set. This helps your grandchild learn that you mean business.

❑ Be careful about making exceptions. If you always give in, your grandchild will learn that the rules don't have to be followed.

❑ Structure = Security. Children need structure in their lives; remember that your grandchild may not have had much structure before coming to live with you, and may not be used to it.

NO GRANDCHILDREN OF YOUR OWN?

You might be surprised to find out that there are still plenty of opportunities for you to work with children. Even if you do have grandchildren of your own, you may still want to lend a hand or an ear to other children in your community, as a "surrogate" grandparent.

Depending on the level of the commitment you want to make, you have several options:

❑ **Volunteer at a local school or hospital**, where your many years of experience will be your most valuable asset. Your work can be in almost any capacity—teaching, counseling, discussing, or simply sharing ideas and thoughts with today's youth. To arrange this, you can contact any local volunteer clearinghouse, or the **Corporation for National Service**, which runs both the National Senior Service Corps and the Retired Senior Volunteer Program.

❑ **Family Friends** program of the National Council on the Aging. This federally-sponsored program recruits older people to provide respite for families with seriously ill children, often leading to a grandparent-grandchild type relationship between the child and the volunteer. As a Family Friend, you agree to spend a certain amount of time with the sick child, to relieve the immediate family of their 24-hour commitment to their loved one.

❑ If you are willing to make a more serious commitment, you might want to consider applying to the U.S. government's **Peace Corps** or **Vista** programs. With the Peace Corps, you can to work abroad with children, teaching anything from personal hygiene and the harvesting of crops to language and communication skills. Vista offers similar programs within the United States.

❑ There are other opportunities, all available to you for the asking. Contact any of the organizations listed in the box, "Resources for Grandparents," on page 116.

RESOURCES FOR GRANDPARENTS

National Council on the Aging
409 Third Street, SW, Suite 200
Washington, DC 20024
Telephone: (202) 479-1200
  Sponsors the Family Friends program,
  which recruits older people to provide
  respite for families with sick children.

Grandparent Information Center
c/o American Association of Retired Persons
601 E Street, NW
Washington, DC 20049
Telephone: (202) 434-2296
  Offers information and support to
  grandparents raising grandchildren.

Corporation for National Service
Senior Services Division
1201 New York Avenue, NW
Washington, DC 20525
Telephone: (800) 424-8867
www.seniorcorps.org
  Sponsors the Senior Companion Program,
  Retired Senior Volunteer Program, and
  Foster Grandparent Program.

The National Parent Information
Telephone: (800) 583-4235
www.npin.org
  Advice for parents regarding children.

Your local church, synagogue, library and social services agency will
have additional information on resources in your community.

AGING PARENTS

As you advance in years, not only will you have new grandchildren with whom to contend, but your own parents who may be in increasing need of your help.

As a growing number of Americans become involved in caring for their aging parents, life care decisions and availability of support services become serious concerns. The challenges facing those caring for their aging parents on a day to day basis are many:

❑ Stress-related illnesses are common for the caretaker. Be aware of signs of depression. Look for professional advice, if needed.

❑ Delegate responsibilities if at all possible, and accept help from others. Suggest specific ways by which those who offer assistance can be effective.

❑ Learn all you can about your loved one's condition

❑ Consider new technologies and therapies to help create independence.

❑ Ask other caregivers how they do it and learn from their experience by sharing stories of your difficult times. Many receive strength in knowing that others have faced the same challenge.

We are living longer, and so are our parents. With age can come difficult, sensitive problems of illness, memory loss, need for constant care. This becomes particularly urgent when only one parent is alive or competent. Many of us live at a distance, sometimes thousands of miles, from our parents.

As we plan for ourselves and our children, so must we discuss and plan with our parents while they are active and healthy. Preparing now can give you and your parents the peace of mind that comes from knowing that you will be able to provide the help they may need.

Simple steps you take while your parents are healthy and active can ensure that no matter how far apart you live, you'll be prepared in an emergency.

START TALKING NOW

Start talking. It may not be easy to tackle the touchy subjects of aging and sickness by long-distance telephone. But whether you talk on the phone or in person, it's vital that you understand what your parents want and need, and how you can help.

Establish a communications network. Meet the people in your parent's life—friends, neighbors, clergy, doctors and financial advisor, and exchange phone numbers. Make sure that you and your parents' most trusted friend have keys to the house.

Ease monthly bookkeeping. You can arrange to have utility and housing bills automatically debited from your parents' checking account, or sign up for programs that notify you if payments are missed.

To set up direct deposit of Social Security benefits, call (800) 772-1213.

Take inventory. Both you and your parents should know what assets exist. Learn where to find the paperwork on brokerage accounts, investments and pensions, as well as legal documents such as titles and wills. Talk about which assets can be tapped for assisted living or nursing home care, e.g. home equity or cash value life insurance.

Assess insurance coverage. Neither Medicare nor Medigap policies pay more than a fraction of the cost of assisted living facilities or expensive nursing home care; some long-term care policies pay for both, but buying coverage gets more expensive as your parents grow older.

CHECK ON AVAILABLE COVERAGE

Your parents may become eligible for Medicaid, but to qualify, most assets must be depleted or transferred at least 36 months before entering a nursing home. Each state has its own rules regarding income and asset limits. Call (800) 638-6833 for referral to the state office you need.

For a free booklet explaining how much Medicare will pay for doctors, hospitals and other providers, call (800) 772-1213. (See page 67)

PREPARE NOW FOR TOMORROW

Prepare for a crisis. Be sure your parents have a durable power of attorney, which gives someone they choose the authority to handle their financial affairs. (They may prefer a so-called springing durable power of attorney, which would take effect only if they become incapacitated.) Establish durable power of attorney for health care or health care proxy; name someone to make medical decisions on their behalf; draft a living will, spelling out their wishes regarding life support. Be certain, also, that they have a current will.

HOME CARE CONCERNS

It is estimated that as many as seven million people receive home health care through agencies or private arrangements. The reason is simple: more people are reaching old age and almost nobody wants to go to a nursing home if there is a way to stay in their own home. It is also less expensive.

But there are problems. Federal and state rules that govern care in nursing homes don't apply in private homes. The industry is growing so fast and the demand for workers is so fierce that some less desirable individuals have entered the field. In most states, safeguarding regulations are inadequate.

Check all references. Ask doctors for referrals. Don't take the agency's word if you hire through an agency. And once you've hired someone, be wary. **Don't give any caregiver access to the patient's funds. Don't write blank checks. And keep a close eye on bank statements and credit cards.** Consider having copies of bills mailed to a third party. As a rule, no caregiver, unless bonded, should deal with a patient's finances.

Finally, make sure care is monitored by a relative or friend. Signs of physical abuse, such as unexplained bumps or bruises, are obvious. Accidents happen, but repeated instances should raise concern. Psychological abuse is tougher to spot, but if a patient becomes withdrawn or starts changing established routines, a closer look may be in order.

CARING FOR PARENTS

For referrals to some 4,800 state and local elder-care information and service providers, call the Eldercare Locator at (800) 677-1116, weekdays from 9:00 am to 8:00 pm, Eastern Standard Time. The Eldercare Locator can also give you telephone numbers for adult daycare and respite services, Medicare and Medigap information, tax assistance for the elderly and more.

The local church or synagogue which your parent attends or is in the neighborhood might recommend a fellow parishioner who, on a full or part time basis, could be helpful to your parent.

FOR MORE INFORMATION...

The following free publications may prove helpful:

❑ *Stay at Home, a Guide to Long Term Care and Housing D 14986*

Write: AARP
601 E Street, NW
Washington, DC 20049
Or call: (202) 434-2277

❑ *How to Choose a Homecare Provider*

❑ *Find a Homecare or Hospice Agency*

Write: National Association for Home Care
228 7th St SE
Washington, DC 20003
www.nahc.org

FOR DIRECT DEPOSIT OF SOCIAL SECURITY BENEFITS

(800) 772-1213

AREA AGENCY ON AGING

To find the Area Agency on Aging (AAA) branch of the Federal Administration on Aging office nearest you, contact (202) 619-0724 or www.aoa.gov.

These AAAs administer and support a wide range of community-based services for the elderly, such as:

❑ Adult day care

❑ Group meals

❑ Legal assistance

❑ Senior center programs

❑ "Meals on Wheels"

❑ Visiting homemakers

❑ Chore services

❑ Friendly visiting

❑ Home health services

❑ Respite care for families

Prepared with the assistance of the New York City Department of Aging.

WHO SHOULD BE VACCINATED	WHAT	WHEN
People over 65	Influenza (flu)	Annually, before early November
People over 65 or with respiratory disease or weakened immune system	Pneumonia	Once in a lifetime If vaccinated before 1984 you may need a booster.
All adults	Tetanus/Diphtheria	Every 10 years

THE YEARS AHEAD

The National Institute of Health reports that most people are living longer and, when older, enjoying life much more.

Not too many years ago, there was an unfortunate concept that things ended abruptly at retirement age, 65 for most Americans, because, "one was old" at that age. We now know that in today's culture that is nonsense.

The truth of the matter is that if you reach age 65, you will have anywhere from 15 to 19 or more years of life ahead of you. As a male, you can expect to live to about 80 and as a female at least to 84.

The longevity today has prompted the National Institute of Health to note that there are three distinct "ages" after 65, roughly a decade apart and each with its different characteristics. In looking ahead to retirement, or if retired and planning for later years, it is interesting to consider the NIH findings.

According to the National Institute of Health:

The first "age"—from 65 to 75—is likely to show no substantial decline in capabilities. The NIH calls this period "young old," a continuation of midlife with only a slight drop in ability to take hikes, play golf or tennis or engage in other accustomed physical activities.

There are reams of data to demonstrate that when you are in your 60's or early 70's your ability to recall, remember, to reason, to calculate numbers will be virtually identical.

Some changes begin to show up in the second "age" from 75 to 85. Lives begin to slow down. We become less confident than we were before age 75.

After age 85 people concentrate more on making their lives comfortable and happy by relaxing more but remaining active by spending time with their friends, children and grandchildren.

IN CONCLUSION

Retirement is a time of change, growth, and adjustment. Sounds like a difficult time, doesn't it? Perhaps, but the best way to turn apprehension into confidence is by planning.

We hope that this book has helped you, and that you are looking forward to retirement with anticipation, good humor…and plans that are right for you.

Some final advice which we appreciate:

AFTER SEVENTY …

Pamper the body,
   Prod the soul
Accept limitations,
   But play a role
Withdraw from the front,
   But stay in the fight
Avoid isolation,
   Keep in sight
Beware of reminiscing,
   Except to a child
To forgetting proper names,
   Be reconciled
Refrain from loquacity,
   Be crisp and concise
And regard self-pity
   As a cardinal vice.
    — *Oliver Higgins Prouty*

HELP YOURSELF — HELP OTHERS

Cooperative Extension is a national education system that serves every county in the country. The staff is ready and anxious to provide solutions to many of the problems faced by all of us today. In addition to serving agricultural clientele, Extension employees have the expertise to help individuals help themselves, improve problem- solving skills of citizens and communities and help youth become good citizens and leaders in their communities.

Contact your Cooperative Extension office for information about any of the following areas. If you need information about a subject that is not shown, it is likely the Extension employees will be able to provide the information or refer you to another reliable provider of the needed information.

- Community Economic Development
- Consumer Horticulture Information
- Consumer Resource Management (Budgeting, Recordkeeping)
- Emergency Preparedness
- Food Safety, Processing and Home Preservation
- 4-H Youth Development Programs
- Home-Based Business Education
- Home Repairs
- Lawn Care and Landscaping
- Master Gardening
- Nutrition Information (Wellness, Disease Risks)
- Pest Management
- Residential Property Management
- Vegetable and Fruit Production and Preservation
- Volunteer Leadership Development
- Water Quality
- Youth-at-Risk Programs

If you have an interest in any of these topics (and many others) Extension offers an opportunity to learn and to volunteer. More than 3,000,000 of your friends and neighbors do volunteer work every year. You may offer the benefit of your skills and experience, for example, to young people through 4-H programs. While giving to others as an Extension volunteer, you can continue your own personal growth and development by learning the latest research-based information in an area of interest to you.

Most information from Cooperative Extension is free of charge. However, there may be nominal charges for printed materials or services.

The telephone number for the Cooperative Extension office in your county or city can be found in your telephone book in the blue pages (county section) or the white pages. Their internet address is http://www.reeusda.gov.

FOR MORE INFORMATION

GOVERNMENT PUBLICATIONS: For a free listing of publications for sale write: Superintendent of Documents, U.S. Government Printing Office, 710 N Capitol St NW, Washington DC 20401 or www.access.gpo.gov/su_docs.

For your free copy of the Consumers Information Catalog, listing over 200 consumer publications, send a postcard to: Consumers Information, Handbook, Pueblo, CO 81009 or www.pueblo.gsa.gov.

EXERCISE: The President's Council on Physical Fitness has prepared a guide, *Walking for Exercise and Pleasure,* that includes illustrated warm-up exercises and advice on how far, how fast, and how often to walk for best results. Send $1 to Consumer Information Center, Pueblo, CO 81009.

PENSIONS: For general information about pensions, write to AARP, Fulfillment Department, at 601 E Street, NW, Washington, DC 20049 and ask for publication D-13533, *Your Pension Plan, A Guide to Getting Through the Maze.*

If your employer can't furnish a copy of your pension plan's annual statement, you can get one from the U.S. Department of Labor. Call 1-202-219-8771. You'll need to know your employer's name, address, and federal tax identification number (it should be on your W-2 wage statement), and the name of the pension plan. Cost: 15¢ a page.

DEBT PROBLEMS: The non-profit Consumer Credit Counseling Service, with over 600 offices nationwide, offers free or low-cost budget planning and assistance in working out financial difficulties. Check local yellow pages, call toll-free (1-800-388-2227) or write to the National Foundation for Consumer Credit, 38505 Country Culb Dr, Suite 210 Farmington Hills, MI 48331 or www.debthelpnow.com.

FINANCIAL PLANNERS: If you need a financial planner (see page 12), you can find one through two industry associations. The National Association of Personal Financial Advisors will send you a list of its members in your area. They are fee-only planners who have at least two years' experience and at least one professional designation. Call or write NAPFA at 355 W Dundee Road, Suite 200 Buffalo Grove, IL 60089, 1-888-333-6659 or www.napfa.org.

The International Association for Financial Planning will send you a free list of planners who have demonstrated experience and knowledge of the profession. For a copy, write to IAFP, 5775 Glenridge Drive NE, Suite B300, Atlanta, GA 30328-5364 or call 1-800-945-4237 or www.iafp.org.

COLLEGE AID: For a worksheet to help figure out how much financial aid your child would qualify for, ask a high school guidance office for the College Board's free brochure, "Meeting College Costs."

The Federal Student Aid Information Center has a free booklet, *The Student Guide.* You can order it by calling toll-free, 1-800-433-3243, or by writing to the Center at P.O. Box 84, Washington, DC 20044 or www.ed.gov.

INSURANCE: For free copies of the Insurance Consumer's Bill of Rights and Responsibilities, by the Consumer Insurance Interest Group, write to the National Association of Professional Insurance Agents, 400 N. Washington Street, Alexandria, Virginia 22314.

For a brochure providing consumer information on life insurance, write to the American Council of Life Insurance, Company Services, 1001 Pennsylvania Ave., NW, 5th Floor South, Washington, DC 20004-2599.

A consortium of life, health, property and casualty insurers has a toll-free insurance help line. You can reach it at: 1-800-942-4242.

INDEX: LOOK IT UP

NOTES

NOTES